PER
ARDUA
AD
ASTRA

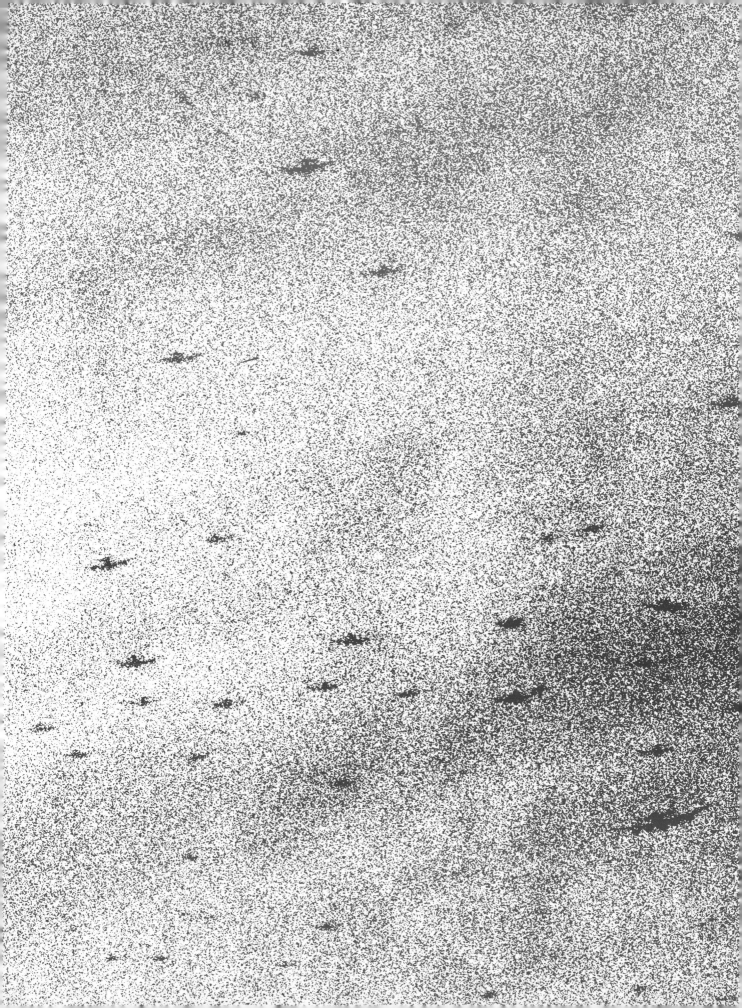

PER ARDUA AD ASTRA

SEVENTY YEARS OF THE RFC & THE RAF

MICHAEL DONNE & SQUADRON LEADER CYNTHIA FOWLER

Frederick Muller Limited
London

4 PER ARDUA AD ASTRA

Acknowledgements

The authors and publishers gratefully acknowledge the assistance of the following companies and organisations who have provided the pictures for this volume:

British Aerospace: Pages 16 (top), 17 (top), 18, 19, 20, 25, 28, 31, 32 (top and bottom), 35 (top and bottom), 38 (top), 41, 43, 46, 72 (top), 74 (top), 75 (bottom), 79 (top and bottom), 80 (top), 82 (top and bottom), 86 (bottom), 115 (top and bottom), 130 opposite, 132, 134 (top), 135 (bottom and opposite), 136 (top and bottom), 137 (top and bottom), 138 (top), 139, 141, 143, 153, 154, 155, 156 (top), 176 (top and bottom).

Central Office of Information: Page 134 (Opposite above).

Imperial War Museum: Pages 84 (right/below), 85, 87, 88, 89, 90, 91, 92, 94, 95, 97, 99, 100, 101, 102, 103, 104, 105, 106, 107, 108, 109, 110 (opposite), 111 (opposite above), 114, 120, 122, 123, 124, 127, 128, 129, 130.

Royal Aircraft Establishment, Farnborough: Pages 12, 13, 14 (top and bottom), 15, 16 (bottom), 21, 22, 26 (top and bottom), 27, 29, 30 (top), 34 (top), 42 (bottom).

Rolls Royce: Pages 17, 41, 64, 66, 67, 68, 137 (middle), 142, 156 (bottom).

Royal Air Force
1. *Air Historical Branch*: Pages 32, 34, 35, 37, 38, 40, 43 (above), 45, 46, 47, 48, 49 (left), 50, 51, 52 (opposite), 53, 54, 55, 57, 58, 59, 60, 61, 70, 71, 71 (opposite), 72, 73, 74, 75, 77, 78, 80 (right), 81, 82, 111 (opposite below), 115, 134 (below), 135 (left), 136, 137 (top), 137 (bottom), 138 (right), 138 (below), 139, 140, 141, 145, 146, 147, 150, 152, 155 (above), 156 (top), 157, 159, 160, 161, 163, 163 (opposite), 164, 167, 168, 169, 171 (above), 172, 173, 175, 176, 177, 178, 179, 180, 181, 183, 184, 185, 186, 187, 188.
2. *Joint School of Photography, RAF Cosford*: Pages 39, 49 (below), 60 (right), 94 (above), 117.

Short Brothers: Pages 80 (bottom), 112.

First published in Great Britain 1982 by Frederick Muller Limited, Dataday House, Alexandra Road, Wimbledon SW19.

Copyright © Michael Donne and Cynthia Fowler 1982

The publishers gratefully acknowledge the assistance of the Royal Air Force

A proportion of the proceeds of this book is being donated to the Royal Air Forces Association.

Donne, Michael and Fowler, Cynthia
  Per Ardua ad Astra
  1. Great Britain. *Royal Air Force* – History
  I. Title
  358.4'00941   UG635.G7

ISBN 0-584-11022-7

Printed in Great Britain by The Fakenham Press Ltd., Norfolk

Contents

Foreword

The history of air power, when measured against that of land and sea power, is short. Indeed it is precisely because we have so little aviation history upon which to draw that the scope for misconception about air power is so great. In Britain, we were fortunate, though, to have men of vision and foresight like Churchill and Trenchard who saw from the outset that aircraft had a unique capacity for carrying the war to the enemy.

As technology has advanced so has the effectiveness of air power, so that it has exerted an influence on warfare out of all proportion to its tender years. Today that influence is all pervasive.

In this book – which marks the 70th Anniversary of the formation of the Royal Flying Corps – Michael Donne, the doyen of Fleet Street defence and air correspondents, admirably fills a gap in our knowledge by tracing graphically the birth and development of air power in Britain and of the Royal Air Force and its tasks today.

Air Chief Marshal Sir Michael Beetham, GCB, CBE, DFC, AFC, ADC – Chief of the Air Staff

Preface

> ". . . . If people forget, they bring war on themselves.
> After many years, they will ask for disarmament, so they
> can raise their standard of living. Movies and radio should
> remind them and future generations of what happened . . .
> to keep this danger in everyone's mind so that we can never
> be caught on the wrong foot again – so that our children
> will have a chance to live."
>
> *Wing Commander Guy Gibson, VC, DSO and bar,
> DFC and bar, Officer Commanding No. 617 (The
> Dam Busters) Squadron, written after the Dam
> Busters Raid May 1943.*

THIS BOOK ORIGINATED in a lunch-time conversation with Air Commodore Dan Honley, Director of Public Relations for the RAF, when we were discussing ways of commemorating the 70th anniversary of the formation of the Royal Flying Corps in the spring of 1912.

There have been many books on the RFC and the RAF, and this one is not intended to be definitive, for there will be many more. Rather, it is intended to be an encapsulation, telling as much in pictures as in words about how things happened, and what life in the Service was like. Inevitably, much has had to be omitted, but the authors hope that what is said at least helps to give the flavour of the Service through some of the most exciting, if turbulent, decades of our recent history.

The joint authors' thanks are due to many, both inside and outside the RAF – to Air Commodore Dan Honley and his team in the RAF Public Relations Department; to Air Commodore Henry Probert and his team at the RAF Air Historical Branch; and to Bob Lawrie and Brian Kervell at the Royal Aircraft Establishment, Farnborough – all of whom gave immense advice and encouragement. Without them, the book could never have been tackled, let alone achieved.

Michael Donne in particular would like to thank all those in the aerospace industry who helped with pictures and advice, and particularly Robert Gardner and his team in British Aerospace. He would also like particularly to thank his co-author, Squadron Leader Cynthia Fowler, who spent many weary hours digging out pictures and writing captions.

London, 1981.

Genesis

Pre-1912

1

MILITARY AERONAUTICS in Britain began with balloons. Hot-air ballooning had started in France in the late eighteenth century with the Montgolfier brothers. Throughout the nineteenth century ballooning achieved some military respectability, especially in the American Civil War. On the Continent it was used to maintain communications with beleaguered cities, as in the Siege of Paris in the Franco-Prussian War. Ballooning also became a pastime for the well-to-do. In Britain, official interest was by comparison, miniscule. It was left to a handful of interested Army officers, mostly in the Royal Engineers and Royal Artillery, to explore the potential of hydrogen balloons. Some of this 'aerostation' was paid for out of their own pockets.

An Army Balloon Equipment Store was first established at Woolwich in 1878, and a certain Captain Templer of the Middlesex Militia was appointed Instructor in Ballooning to the Royal Engineers, with a grant of £150 to build Britain's first military balloon, *Pioneer*. The Balloon Equipment Store went to Chatham in 1882, where a small balloon factory, depot and school were set up, again with Templer as the driving force.

From this point on, James Lethbridge Brooke Templer figures prominently in the story of Army ballooning and later also in airship development. Balloons were used on active service in the Sudan in 1885, and to observe the annual Army manoeuvres at Aldershot in 1889. In 1890 a Balloon Section of the Royal Engineers was formed at Aldershot, with the Balloon Factory and School following from Chatham in 1892. Balloons in the British Army really came into their own during the Boer War, however, when they gave valuable service in Natal at Ladysmith, in the Transvaal, and in the Orange Free State. They provided observation for ground artillery during several famous battles, including those at Zwarts Kop, Magersfontein, Paardeberg, Bloemfontein and Driefontein. Colonel Templer – when he was able to tear himself

A man-lifting kite, showing the basket with the passengers in it, rising from Balloon Square, Aldershot, around 1904–5, prior to the move of the Royal Engineers' Balloon Section to Farnborough in 1906.

away from driving traction engines, to which he was addicted as a means of Army transport – perfected the art of military ballooning in South Africa. The result was that by the end of the war, the Army was not only much keener on ballooning than it had been before, but also was far ahead of any other nation in the use of such craft. Templer remained with the Balloon Factory and School until 1906, only two years before he finally left the Army in 1908. He had been the great pioneer of ballooning in the Army for thirty years, and thus rightly can be described as one of the founding fathers of British military aeronautics. More than any other

individual at that time, he laid the foundations of what was to follow, although he never had any direct involvement in or influence upon the development of manned, fixed-wing aeroplanes.

At that time, the manned, heavier-than-air aeroplane was virtually unknown in Europe, or indeed for that matter in the United States. The Wright Brothers' epoch-making flight on 17 December 1903, at Kill Devil Hills, near Kitty Hawk on the North Carolina coast, had passed almost unnoticed in the international press. Even where it had been mentioned, there were very few who really appreciated the implications of it, while the Wrights themselves did not seek or encourage publicity. As a result, the British War Office, in a report of 1903–4, only recommended further work on balloons and the development of a dirigible (steerable) airship. This led to the creation of the 'Balloon Companies' of the Royal Engineers in April 1905, and eventually to the creation of the Balloon School at Farnborough, Hampshire, under Colonel John Capper, who replaced Templer as Commandant in April 1906. This School, of which Capper also became the Superintendent, was established at a new 'Army Balloon Factory' at Farnborough, the precursor of today's Royal Aircraft Establishment which stands on the same site.

It was at Farnborough, under Colonel Capper, that the work

An Army balloon being inflated, around the early part of this century. It is made from 'goldbeater's skin', a material derived from oxen's intestines, and with a low permeability to gases, even hydrogen. Up to and including the giant airship Hindenberg, goldbeater's skin was used to make the gasbags for airships. The type of balloon shown was common at that time in the Army Balloon Section.

Above. *The airship* Nulli Secundus II *being handled out of the 'Beta' shed at Farnborough early on Friday 24 July 1908. The craft was unsuccessful, with a life of only one month, in which it made three flights.*

Right. *The engine of airship Beta I, around 1910. The system, suspended beneath the airship, is strangely reminiscent of the 'Flying Bedstead' rig for vertical take-off research of the late 1950s.*

Col. J. L. B. Templer,
Superintendent, 1878-1906

Col. J. E. Capper, C.B., R.E.,
Superintendent, 1906-1909

Lt. Col. M. J. P. O'Gorman,
Superintendent, 1909-1916

Sir Henry Fowler, K.B.E.,
Superintendent, 1916-1918

W. Sydney Smith,
Superintendent, 1918-1926;
Chief Superintendent, 1926-1928

begun by Templer on the development of Britain's first military airship, the *Nulli Secundus I*, was completed. This craft first flew in September 1907, and in a short career made one of the most famous flights attempted up to that time – over London on 5 October, circling St Paul's Cathedral. Both Colonel Capper and a certain 'Colonel' Cody were on board. After a flight of three hours and twenty-five minutes, in which they covered fifty miles (80.47 km), they were obliged to land at the Crystal Palace in South London, because unfavourable winds prevented a return direct to Farnborough. The flight generated enormous public excitement.

Even while airship development continued, with the *Nulli Secundus II* emerging in 1908, followed by *Baby* and *Beta I*, both in 1909, the day of the military balloon and airship in Britain was already beginning to wane, although airship development was continued until well after the end of the First World War.

One of the prime movers in this trend away from airships to manned, powered aircraft was a flamboyant American, 'Colonel' (he was never officially commissioned into the British Army) Samuel Franklin Cody, a public entertainer who became enamoured of kite flying in the early years of this century after he had settled in England. He developed man-carrying kites, which he demonstrated first to the Royal Navy, and then to the Army, for

The men who virtually founded British military aviation at the Army Balloon Factory and its successors are shown in this montage photograph. They are from, left to right, Colonel J. L. B. Templer (Superintendent, 1878–1906); his successor, Colonel J. E. Capper (1906–1909); who was followed in turn by Lieut. Col. Mervyn O'Gorman (1909–1916), who was largely responsible for steering the Army Balloon Factory towards manned military aircraft. He was followed by Sir Henry Fowler (1916–1918), who in turn was succeeded by W. Sydney Smith (1918–1928).

Below is shown Britain's second airship, the Nulli Secundus II *flying over the Army Balloon Factory, as it then was, on 24 July 1908. In the background is the original airship shed.*

Alliott Verdon-Roe was one of the great pioneers of aviation in Britain, responsible for a long line of military, and later also civil aircraft. In 1908, he was the first man to fly (in a series of hops) over British soil in a British aircraft using a British engine, but his achievement was never officially recognised. Colonel Cody (an American) is always credited with the first official manned powered aircraft flight in Britain, with J. T. Moore-Brabazon credited as the first British citizen to fly (gaining Royal Aero Club Certificate No. 1), at Leysdown on the Isle of Sheppey in 1909.

'Colonel' Samuel Franklin Cody, an American entertainer turned aviator, whose activities did much to help create a climate of public opinion in favour of manned, powered flying in the early years of this century.

observation purposes. He eventually became Kite Instructor to the Balloon Section in 1905 and Chief Kite Instructor in 1906. Then his interests swung more towards powered aircraft flying, and he began to develop his own aircraft, achieving the first officially credited, manned, heavier-than-air aircraft flight in England on 16 October 1908. Alliott Verdon-Roe had in fact made a series of 'hops' at Brooklands motor-racing circuit at Weybridge, thereby unofficially becoming the first man to fly over British soil in a British aircraft powered by a British engine. Cody crashed his aircraft, however, after achieving a flight of 1,390 feet (424 metres). The next year, as a result of a policy change, his Government contract was not renewed so he left the Army Balloon Factory to experiment with his aeroplanes near Farnborough, on Laffan's Plain. He did so well that eventually he won the Army's military aeroplane trials in 1912, but sadly he was killed with a passenger in a crash on Laffan's Plain on 7 August 1913, when the last of several aircraft which he had built himself broke up in the air.

Much has been made of Cody, and he was indeed a public figure of considerable idiosyncracy. But he was important only in that he helped to create a climate of opinion in favour of powered aircraft, along with the work of the many other aviation pioneers at that time, whose efforts were much more seriously directed to the long-term development of powered flying.

Above. *Geoffrey de Havilland, seen with Frank Hearle, in the early days of their work on manned, powered aircraft. De Havilland and Hearle both went on to become founders and directors of the de Havilland Aircraft Company, one of the most famous British civil and military aircraft manufacturers.*

Left. *The Hon. Charles Stewart Rolls, in one of his early flying machines. A pioneer motorist, balloonist and powered aviator, he was co-founder with Frederick Henry Royce of the famous Rolls-Royce company in 1906. Rolls was killed at a Bournemouth flying meeting in July 1910.*

Thomas Sopwith was another
early pioneer whose activities
eventually became closely linked
with British civil and military
aviation, through the Hawker
company, named after his own
chief test pilot Harry Hawker –
whom Sopwith taught to fly but
who became better at it than
Sopwith himself. Above, *Sopwith
is seen aloft on his first solo flight
in a Howard Wright monoplane
in 1910, and* right, *with one of
his own early machines.*

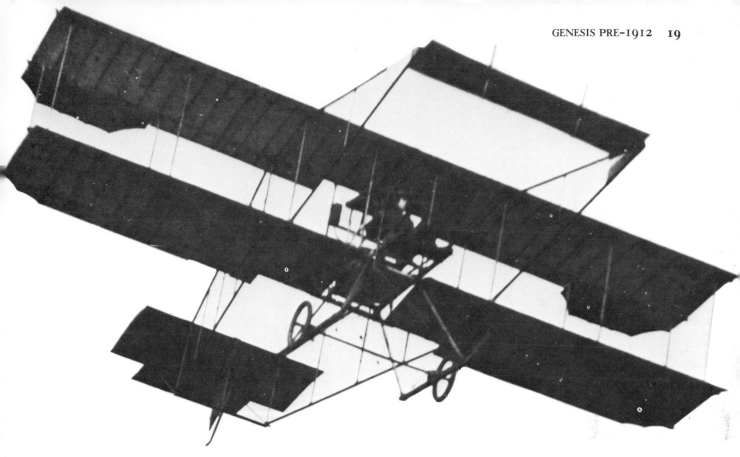

Those other pioneers, apart from Alliott Verdon-Roe, included the three Short brothers (Horace, Eustace and Oswald) who had become the first manufacturers of aircraft in the world, having gained the licence after 1908 to build the Wright Flyer in the UK, first at Shellbeach in the Isle of Sheppey (the Royal Aero Club's first flying ground) and later at Rochester. The Hon. C. S. Rolls, co-founder with Henry Royce of Rolls-Royce (initially motor-car manufacturers and only subsequently becoming involved in aero-engines late in 1914) was flying at Sheppey in 1909, having deserted ballooning for manned powered flight. He was subsequently killed in an air crash at the Bournemouth flying meeting in 1910.

Several other young aviation pioneers were also busy around this time, all of whom were later to be intimately connected with the history of the Royal Flying Corps and the Royal Air Force. They included Robert Blackburn, who first flew his own aircraft from a Yorkshire beach in the spring of 1909, and Geoffrey de Havilland, who first flew in December 1909. Thomas Sopwith had flown in balloons in 1908, but learned to fly a powered aircraft in 1910, opening his own flying school at Brooklands in 1912. There he trained several keen young airmen, later destined to become famous, including a Major Hugh Trenchard. Sopwith also began to build his own aircraft in a converted skating rink at Kingston-on-Thames in 1912.

Sir George White, a rich and successful Bristol tramways and omnibus pioneer, set up his own aircraft company, the British and

Geoffrey de Havilland's second aircraft, in September 1910, which was really his first successful machine: his initial effort in 1909 had crashed soon after take-off, with only its engine (which he had also designed) salvageable. Although working initially alone, he joined Mervyn O'Gorman at Farnborough, but left to work privately again with the Aircraft Manufacturing Company at Hendon in 1914. Nevertheless, his influence on Farnborough designs was felt for years after he had left.

Sir George White, the Bristol tramways and omnibus pioneer who founded the British and Colonial Aeroplane Company, later renamed the Bristol Aeroplane Company. The 'Bristol' name has been associated with many famous fighters, bombers and engines throughout the history of military aviation in Britain. The company was merged some years ago to form the British Aircraft Corporation, now in turn part of British Aerospace.

Colonial (later Bristol) Aeroplane Company, in February 1910. Vickers, already at that time famous as an armaments manufacturer, initially built airships but opened a flying school at Brooklands in 1911, and set up an aircraft factory at Erith in Kent, moving it to Brooklands in 1915. Sir W. G. Armstrong Whitworth, also a noted armaments manufacturer, came into aircraft design and construction around this time, after initially developing airships. Frederick Handley Page began to build his own gliders at Barking Creek in 1909, swiftly moving into powered aircraft with *Bluebird* in 1910.

While all these events were taking place, the atmosphere at Farnborough was changing dramatically. In 1909, following a reorganisation initiated by Lord Haldane, then the Minister for War, Mervyn O'Gorman, an engineer by training, although he also held Dublin degrees in Science and Classics, succeeded Colonel Capper as head of the Balloon Factory. Capper remained head of the Balloon School. It was to be a revolutionary change. O'Gorman was no balloonist or airship enthusiast. He was a manned aircraft protagonist of strong personality, and he was determined to change things his way, no matter how difficult it might be. His abrasive, dynamic character prevailed, and it is largely due to him that Farnborough expanded rapidly, moving away from balloons, kites and airships into manned aeroplanes. He appointed as his chief engineer Frederick Michael Green, from the Daimler company, and it was on Green's advice that O'Gorman also appointed as chief designer and test pilot the young, impecunious Geoffrey de Havilland, who had just designed his own first successful aircraft, but could not afford to continue.

It was one of the most far-sighted things O'Gorman ever did. For under de Havilland and Green, the entire direction and tempo of work at Farnborough changed. The Factory began to develop both aircraft and aero-engines, and in the space of a few short years it became the primary home of military aircraft development in Britain. A series of designs flowed from it that were to render invaluable service through the First World War, even after Geoffrey de Havilland had left, in 1914, to join G. Holt Thomas at the Aircraft Manufacturing Company at Hendon, from whence came the famous early range of DH designs. The Farnborough designs included the BE (Blériot Experimental tractor biplanes), the BS (Blériot Scout single-seat tractor biplanes, later to become the SE series), the FE (Farman Experimental pusher-type biplanes), and the RE (Reconnaissance Experimental two-seaters), all of which types and designations were to become familiar to Royal Flying Corps pilots during the war that was looming. To start it all O'Gorman actually bought de Havilland's own first aircraft for £400, and it became the FE-1.

The early official indifference at the War Office to manned

aeroplanes was also crumbling under the pressure of events, but even so, things still moved slowly. In mid-1909, an Advisory Committee for Aeronautics was set up, but it did not achieve very much. During the spring of 1911, an 'Air Battalion' under Major Sir Alexander Bannerman was created, charged with forming 'a body of expert airmen, organised in such a way as to facilitate the formation of units ready to take to the field with troops, and capable of expansion by forming reserve formations'. It became responsible for the training and instruction of men in handling kites, balloons and aeroplanes, and other forms of aircraft. The Air Battalion took over the entire balloon, kite and airship activities of the Royal Engineers, as well as the aircraft activities already under way at the Farnborough Balloon Factory under O'Gorman. The Farnborough establishment now became the Army Aircraft Factory. The creation of what was to become a major aerial fighting force was drawing closer.

The A.V. Roe (Avro) Type E being transported through Manchester in 1910. 'AV' had begun his early attempts to fly at Brooklands motor racing track in Surrey in 1907, but had encountered hostility and transferred temporarily to Lea Marshes and then to Manchester before returning to Brooklands in 1910, where a new attitude in favour of powered aircraft flying prevailed.

Above. *The Army Aircraft Factory (or 'Aerial Works', as it was locally known) as it appeared at Farnborough late in 1911, shortly before the formation of the RFC, showing the remarkably large size of the buildings for that time, when powered aviation was still in its comparative infancy. The factory was still engaged in airship activities, but was moving into powered aircraft under the leadership of Mervyn O'Gorman.*

Opposite. *A copy of the original Royal Warrant founding the Royal Flying Corps. It came into effect a month later on 13 May 1912.*

In 1911, the Government, under Prime Minister Asquith, could no longer ignore the massive increase in activity in powered aircraft going on all round it, both at home and especially on the Continent in France and Germany. Asquith asked the standing sub-committee of the Committee of Imperial Defence, under the chairmanship of Lord Haldane, to study the situation. Its Report was produced in February 1912, and its recommendations, embodied in a White Paper published in April 1912, provided for the amalgamation of the existing small naval and military flying activities into one organisation, to be called 'The Flying Corps'. It was to have five sections – a Military Wing, a Naval Wing, a Reserve, a Central Flying School near Upavon on Salisbury Plain, and the Army Aircraft Factory at Farnborough, which was henceforth to be known as the Royal Aircraft Factory, responsible for the design, development and production of manned aircraft. The latter was something which the rapidly developing private aircraft-manufacturing industry objected to strongly, and, eventually, after considerable intrigue, resulted in Farnborough becoming solely a research and development centre later in the First World War.

King George V approved the title of 'Royal' in March, and on 13 April 1912, the Royal Flying Corps was constituted by Royal Warrant, but the Corps actually came into being on 13 May. The basis of an aerial fighting force had been created, and as events were soon to prove, it was only just in time.

ROYAL WARRANTS

20
Royal
Flying
Corps

Royal Flying Corps (Military Wing)   *No. 130*
1912

GEORGE R.I.

1 WHEREAS WE have approved of the establishment of an aerial
service for naval and military purposes under the designation of the
Royal Flying Corps;

AND WHEREAS it is necessary to form a Military Wing of the
Royal Flying Corps to which officers and men of Our Land Forces
can be appointed; OUR WILL AND PLEASURE is that the Royal
Flying Corps (Military Wing) shall be decreed to be a corps for the
purpose of the Army Act.

Given at Our Court at St James's this 13th day of April, 1912,
in the Second year of Our Reign.

By His Majesty's Command,

HALDANE OF CLOAN

2 Early Days of the RFC
1912–1914

THE DETAILED implementation of the Government's plans for the Royal Flying Corps was entrusted to three very able officers, under the overall control of Colonel J. E. B. Seely, the Under Secretary of State for War. They were Brigadier-General David Henderson, CB, DSO (who became Director of Military Training for the Army in July 1912); Major D. S. MacInnes, RE, of the Committee of Imperial Defence; and Captain Frederick Sykes, a General Staff Officer. Henderson was a 49-year-old veteran of the Boer War, who had been taught to fly by Howard Pixton in 1911 at the Bristol Flying School at Brooklands after only seven days' tuition. He became the first Director-General of Military Aeronautics in September 1913. Sykes had been at one time a member of the Balloon School at Farnborough, and had learned to fly shortly before Henderson, on a Bristol Boxkite.

The initial plan was that military or naval officers, and civilians, who wished to join the Royal Flying Corps should learn to fly at one of the many civilian flying schools then proliferating and win their Royal Aero Club Certificates, thereafter joining the Central Flying School at Upavon for further advanced training. If accepted, they would be given £75 (then a considerable sum) as part of the costs of their civilian training. Provision was made initially for 91 military, 40 naval and 15 civilian pilots to pass through the new CFS every year.

The Government placed an initial order for 25 training aeroplanes. The aim was for the Military Wing of the RFC, under the initial command of Captain Sykes, to build up quickly to seven squadrons of 12 aeroplanes each. The Royal Aircraft Factory at Farnborough was given the task of training air mechanics, rebuilding aeroplanes, building engines and equipment, and undertaking the testing of new aircraft and engines. It also designed and built aircraft initially, but eventually it was to be debarred from this, as a result of representations from the aircraft manufacturers who regarded the Factory's own manufacturing activities as unfair competition.

Virtually all the officers who volunteered from other units of the Army and Navy for service with the nascent RFC were interested solely in manned, heavier-than-air machines, with few seriously interested in either balloons or kites, or even airships. In June, the Central Flying School opened at Upavon, under the command of Captain G. Paine, RN. It was to be maintained at the joint expense of the Army and Navy. Trenchard was second-in-command, and it was here that his famous nickname, 'Boom', was bestowed on him as a result of his resonant and penetrating voice.

Already, there were signs that the Navy was none too happy about becoming too closely involved with the RFC. A particular feature of the early history of the Corps is how the initial suspicions of traditional Corps, such as the Cavalry, slowly turned to a warm recognition of the advantages of aerial reconnaissance and other activities. When the War came, the RFC went to France primarily as part of the Army, and throughout the war Naval interest in aviation was confined to much more limited areas. The Admiralty was slower than the Army to take to flying, although the Royal Naval Air Service, which was created out of the original Naval

A.V. Roe's fourth design, the Triplane IV, completed in September 1910, and used for training many early aviators at the Avro Flying School at Brooklands.

Above. *The Royal visit to
Farnborough in 1914 by King
George V. What are now called
the 'Black Sheds' – they are still
there – are only a few months old.
The famous tree to which 'Colonel'
Cody tethered his early flying
machines is on the right.*

Right. *The first headquarters of
the Royal Flying Corps at
Farnborough, in 1914. The low
building on the right was the
original Balloon Equipment
Store, and is now the museum of
the Royal Aircraft Establishment.*

Wing of the RFC on 1 July 1914, did perform some notable wartime feats. One of these was operating against Zeppelins seeking to attack the UK. The Admiralty had been given part of the task of home defence against air attack (although small numbers of RFC aircraft also shared this role). After the creation of the RNAS, Naval and Military aviation tended to develop along separate lines, until the RFC and RNAS were again amalgamated into the Royal Air Force on 1 April 1918. The Admiralty also preferred to deal directly with the aircraft manufacturers, such as Short Brothers, Vickers, Blackburn, Sopwith, and later Fairey, rather than with the Royal Aircraft Factory. This helps to account for the long association of these companies with the Royal Navy, and with flying-boat development in particular, in the cases of Shorts and Blackburn.

The Admiralty was also particularly successful in stimulating the development of new aero-engines – it was largely due to encouragement from the Admiralty that Henry Royce, the co-founder of Rolls-Royce, began to develop aero-engines for the first time in late 1914, having previously concentrated on motor-cars. It was also during this time, and into the First World War, that many of the famous seaplane stations were set up round Britain's

One of the earliest machines to emerge from the Royal Aircraft Factory in 1914 was the BE-2b. The design was such that a machine gun could not be mounted, and the type had been withdrawn from the Western Front by the autumn of 1915, after 85 had been supplied to the RFC.

The early design of the Avro 504, later to become one of the most famous trainers of the RFC and RAF. Avro's name is on the side, in the tradition of the early aviation pioneers, who were anxious to gain as much publicity for their designs as they could. More than 8,000 Avro 504s in various versions were built during 1914–18, and it remained in service well into the post-war period.

coasts, including Eastchurch, the Isle of Grain, Calshot, Felixstowe, Yarmouth and Cromarty.

It was partly to seek the best aircraft available for future development that the first Army Aircraft Trials were held in August 1912, with General Henderson, Major F. H. Sykes and Mervyn O'Gorman among the judges. The Trials were held at Larkhill on Salisbury Plain, and over 30 aircraft were entered, including designs from Vickers, A. V. Roe, Blériot, Breguet, British Deperdussin, British & Colonial Aeroplane Company (Bristol), Martin-Handasyde, Maurice Farman, French Deperdussin, Handley Page, S. F. Cody and others. Although, under the contest rules, Cody won the first prize of £5,000, his design was deemed unsuitable for development. It was apparent that the Royal Aircraft Factory's own design, the BE-2 tractor-biplane, demonstrated by Geoffrey de Havilland, with Sykes as a passenger, was the better aircraft.

The principal result of the Trials was that the Military Wing of the RFC tended, at least initially, to order its designs from the Royal Aircraft Factory in quantity. One of the most formidable and famous weapons of the First World War, the SE-5 Fighting Scout,

emerged from lessons learned by the Factory's design team as a result of the Trials. Yet another little recognised result was that A. V. Roe, whose initial design, the Type G, failed to win, was nevertheless encouraged to design the eventual Avro 504, a simple, rugged aeroplane that became one of the most famous trainers of all time. It was used by the RFC and eventually also by the RAF well into the 1930s. Countless thousands of RAF pilots were taught to fly on the 504 using the Gosport system initiated by Major Smith-Barry.

In September 1912, the first Army manoeuvres supported by aircraft were held in East Anglia, with some 24 aircraft of various kinds participating. In all, some 7,855 miles (12,641 km) were flown, a formidable total for that time. A memorandum by the Director of Military Operations at the War Office declared: 'There can no longer be any doubt as to the value of airships and aeroplanes in locating an enemy on land and obtaining information which could otherwise only be obtained by force. . . . Though aircraft will probably have several uses in war, their primary duty is searching for information'. It is significant that even at that time, the possibilities of direct air-to-air combat had not yet percolated into the

Making wings at Farnborough in late 1913 or early 1914, involved covering frames with fabric and 'doping' them for tautness. The wings shown are probably for RE-5s and the only FE-6 built, both Factory designs. The shields along the right-hand wall above the lights are the nameplates of scrapped Army balloons.

Building four-bladed, fixed-pitch wooden propellers by hand at Farnborough, probably just prior to the First World War, a highly skilled activity.

minds of those in power at the War Office.

The slow expansion of the RFC continued. In 1913, an experimental branch of the Military Wing was set up to deal with ballooning, kiting, wireless telegraphy, photography, meteorology, bomb-dropping, musketry, gunnery, and artillery co-operation. This was the forerunner of the Aeroplane and Armament Experimental Establishment (AAEE), now at Boscombe Down. The pilots of the RFC began to explore the frontiers of aviation even further, pushing their flimsy aircraft to the limits of their structural endurance, and themselves to the limits of their knowledge and beyond. The first night flight was undertaken in a Maurice Farman biplane from the Military Wing in April 1913, piloted by Lieutenant Cholmondeley, while in November, a non-stop flight of 445 miles (716 km) in 7 hours 20 minutes was carried out by Captain C. A. H. Longcroft in a BE-2 from Montrose to Portsmouth and then to Farnborough, winning the first Britannia Challenge Trophy awarded by the Royal Aero Club. The new service was developing steadily, but even then few in the RFC were aware of the holocaust that lay ahead.

Equipment as worn by the Royal Flying Corps in its early days, showing the strong influence of the Army – the RFC had not then evolved its own distinctive styles of uniform and equipment.

The First World War 1914–1918 and the Birth of the RAF
1918

3

"Now all the youth of England are on fire,
And silken dalliance in the wardrobe lies;
Now thrive the armourers, and honour's thought
Reigns solely in the breast of every man. . . ."
Chorus, *Henry V.*

As the war shadows loomed, the RFC was brought together in June 1914, at Netheravon, in what became known as the 'Concentration Camp'. This meant the concentration of all the RFC's aeroplanes and personnel in one place for the benefit of lectures, discussions and practical flying on tactical exercises, reconnaissance and inter-service co-operation.

By 1914, the RFC had a mixed bag of Henri Farmans, Blériot monoplanes, Avro biplanes, FE-8s and BE-2s. The RFC went to war on 4 August 1914, flying to France for duty with the Expeditionary Force with four squadrons, totalling 105 officers, 63 aeroplanes and 95 units of motor transport, under the command of Brigadier-General Sir David Henderson, with Lt.-Col. F. H. Sykes as his General Staff Officer I (GSOI). The Corps comprised officers from virtually every section of the Army, but especially the Cavalry. Left at home under the command of Lt.-Col. Hugh Trenchard were 116 aeroplanes (described as 'mainly junk'), 41 officers and a few hundred airmen. It was an inauspicious beginning. In fact, in 1914, the total output of aircraft in Britain for the year was only 211. But such was the influence of the war that in the following year, it had risen to 2,093, and rose further to 6,099 in 1916, to 14,168 in 1917, and then to a rate of about 2,000 a month in 1918.

The aerial war in France began sedately enough, belying the ferocity to come. The early days of gentlemanly reconnaissance in support of the Army soon gave way to open combat with two-seaters, in which the observer also fired a machine gun from his

The de Havilland DH-2 of 1915. This single-seat 'pusher' fighter (with its propeller at the rear of the fuselage) was de Havilland's second design to emerge after he had left Farnborough and joined G. Holt Thomas at the Aircraft Manufacturing Company at Hendon. It served widely in France with the Royal Flying Corps until it was superseded in 1917.

Opposite. *Sopwith Salamanders in production at Sopwith's Ham works, near Kingston, in late 1918.*

open cockpit. Casualties mounted swiftly. The war in the air took a vicious turn when a Dutchman working for the Germans called Anthony Fokker invented in 1915 the synchronised machine-gun, firing through the arc of the propeller. Initially installed on a Fokker Eindekker monoplane, this enabled single-seat fighters to be developed, dispensing with the observer/gunner. As a result, the 'Fokker Scourge' emerged, and for a time the Germans had the edge over the RFC, before British technology caught up in 1916 with such aircraft as the Sopwith $1\frac{1}{2}$-Strutter and the de Havilland DH-2. Aerial combat thereafter increased rapidly, with each side bringing in new fighters of greater performance and improved armament. As a result, the tide swung backwards and forwards, and at one stage, the life of an RFC pilot on the Western Front was put at no more than eight days. The worst month was 'Bloody April' in 1917, when the RFC lost 316 officers and men, one fatal casualty for every 92 flying hours, double the average for the year as a whole.

Early in 1917 a new generation of fighters began to emerge on the British side, including the single-seat Sopwith Camel, the two-seat Bristol F-2 and the single-seat SE-5A, which helped to turn the tide in favour of the Allies. By the end of 1917, with the effects of the RFC's new 'Schools of Aerial Fighting' also beginning to show results, the RFC was clearly in the ascendant. By then it had over 3,200 aircraft at its call, and over 121,000 officers and men – and was still growing.

Right. *A Farman aircraft with an experimental gun mounting at Farnborough in June 1913. Following the creation of the Royal Flying Corps, the Factory's work increasingly involved studies into the use of aircraft for combat roles.*

Below. *The era of the Jumbo skirt! A cheerful squad of members of the Women's Royal Air Force, which was established in 1918, along with the RAF itself.*

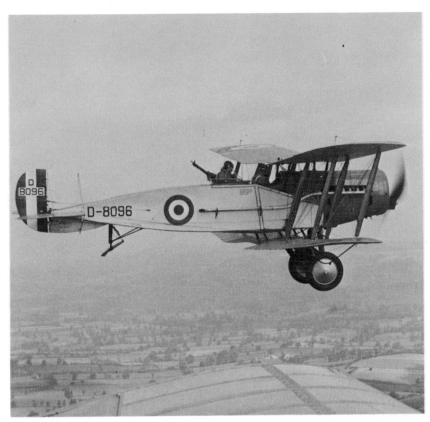

Left. *The Bristol Fighter ('Biff' or 'Brisfit') was one of the most significant fighters of the First World War, with 3,100 built between 1916 and the war's end. Another 1,369 were built before production ended, and it served until the early 1930s, especially overseas in Iraq and India.*

Below. *The DH-4 single-engined two-seat day bomber went into service in March 1917. In the early post-war period, it was converted into a passenger-carrying communications aircraft, the DH-4A, used to ferry VIPs to and from the Paris Peace Conference in 1919.*

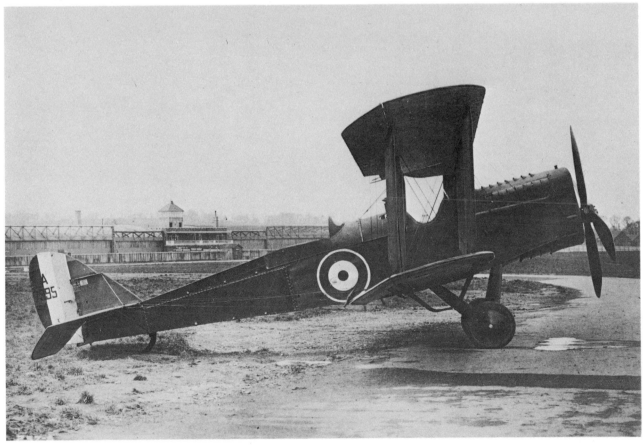

The RFC's tasks included directly aiding the Army in the massive ground battles that occurred throughout the war, strafing and bombing enemy trenches and other positions, and attacking supply lines and artillery positions. It was also engaging in direct air-to-air combat. In these air battles, some of the most stirring episodes in the entire history of aerial warfare occurred, with great 'circuses' of brightly painted aircraft involved, especially on the German side. Thus, the era of the great fighter 'aces' was born, including James McCudden, Albert Ball and Edward Mannock on the British side, all using SE-5As, and Baron Manfred Von Richthofen on the German side, flying the famous red Fokker Triplane.

Casualties, inevitably, were appalling. These mounting losses caused much distress and political activity at home. Progressively, throughout the War, the need to build up the RFC so rapidly put strains on its organisation, and various efforts were made to establish a more coherent command structure. An Air Board had been set up under the presidency of Lord Curzon in May 1916, to try to co-ordinate policy on air matters, but this was none too successful, and it was given limited executive powers, under Lord Cowdray, in December 1916.

King George V inspecting the Royal Flying Corps at war on the Western Front. The aircraft on the left is a Sopwith Camel fighter.

Opposite. 'Standing Orders' for the Women's Royal Air Force, stating bluntly that 'a high standard of behaviour shall be maintained'.

Above. *The de Havilland DH-9 two-seat bomber of 1917, showing the Hucks Starter devised for rapid starting of aircraft engines. The picture shows the great advances made by de Havilland in his designs in just a few years, when compared with the DH-2 of 1915 (p. 32).*

Right. *A Sopwith Pup landing on HMS* Furious, *during aviation trials by the Royal Naval Air Service (which began as the Naval Wing of the RFC).*

A painting of one of the aerial battles over the Western Front in the First World War. The aircraft are German Albatrosses (centre) and a Martinsyde (top left).

Sir Hugh Trenchard as the first Chief of the Air Staff. Lieutenant-General Sir David Henderson was Vice-President of the Air Council.

It was not a very happy arrangement. Trenchard did not get on with Rothermere, and he resigned his post on 12 April 1918. He was replaced by Major-General Sir Frederick Sykes. It could have been a disaster for Trenchard, for he was, after all, a serving senior officer, and such men have no right to resign in war-time. Moreover, in March, it was officially announced that the King had approved the formation of the Royal Air Force, and it came into being on 1 April, merging the Royal Flying Corps and the Royal Naval Air Service. The Women's Royal Air Force was formed the same day.

The bitter political in-fighting continued. Lord Rothermere

The Women's Royal Air Force was set up at the same time as the RAF on 1 April 1918, to take over many administrative and other duties, thus releasing men for combatant duties. The WRAF immediately attracted several thousands of enthusiastic recruits.

resigned on 26 April and was replaced on the 27th by Sir William Weir, who had been Director-General of Aircraft Production in the Ministry of Munitions, and had also been given a seat on the first Air Council. Weir immediately ordered Trenchard back to France, as Commander of the newly-created Independent Force, and there Trenchard stayed, with no clear idea of his own long-term future.

The end of the War was not now very far away. It came on 11 November 1918, after more than four years of exhausting struggle, during which time the RFC and RNAS had borne the brunt of the entire battle in the air. By the end of the war, it was undoubtedly the finest aerial fighting force in the world. On charge to it were 22,647 aircraft of all types, including 3,300 on first-line strength, and 103 airships. There were 133 squadrons and 15 flights

Vickers Vimy bomber production at Morgan's Aircraft Works, near Leighton Buzzard, in 1918, with Rolls-Royce Eagle VIII engines in the foreground. Sub-contracting of aircraft production was common practice in the First World War, in order to achieve rapid maximum output.

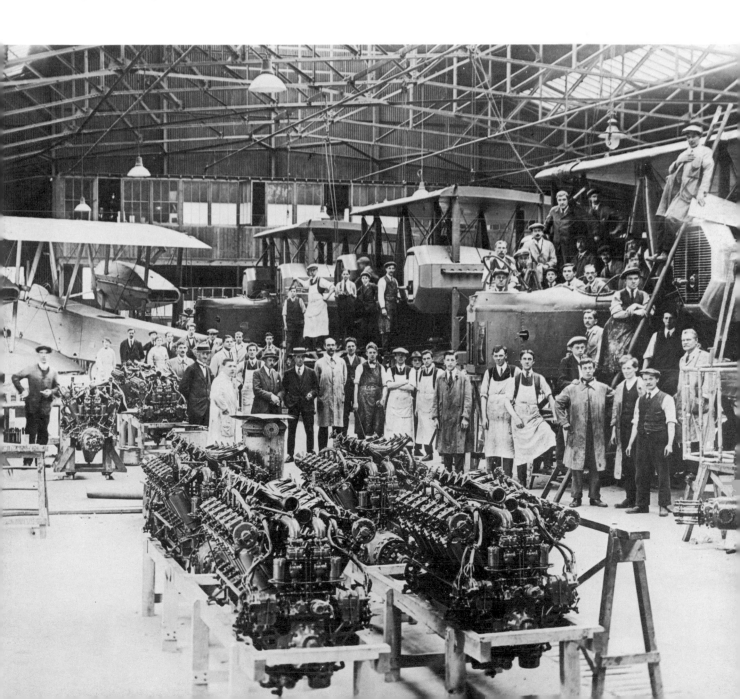

overseas (on the Western Front, in the Middle East, in Italy and in the Mediterranean), and 55 squadrons at home. In addition, there were 75 training squadrons and depots, and 401 aerodromes at home and 274 abroad. The personnel strength was 27,333 officers and 263,837 other ranks, and about 25,000 in the Women's Royal Air Force. The aircraft industry, too, had come a long way, and was producing about 3,500 aeroplanes a month.

The losses, however, had been colossal. Many thousands of aircraft had been destroyed – on both sides, the German losses alone amounting to over 8,000 aircraft. The total casualties for the RFC, the RNAS and latterly also the RAF, from 1914 to 1918, amounted to 4,579 officers and 1,587 men killed, 2,839 officers and 373 men missing or interned (mostly after having been shot down), and 5,369 officers and 1,876 men wounded, again mainly in aerial combat. For although the enemy frequently attacked RFC airfields and bases, these were sufficiently far behind the lines to escape massive bombardment and heavy casualties.

Despite the ravages of war, the newly-born RAF looked forward to a long and illustrious career. Little did its officers and men appreciate that severe difficulties and a long struggle for survival lay just round the corner.

Above. *A Handley Page 0/400 heavy bomber of No. 1 Communications Squadron. Called the 'Bloody Paralyser', the 0/400 became the RAF's standard heavy bomber in the First World War.*

Opposite. *The installation of a Harle searchlight, coupled with two Lewis guns, in an FE-2b at Farnborough, in March 1917. The officer is Lt. W. S. Farren, later Sir William Farren.*

4 Trenchard and the 'Corps d'Elite'

1919–1929

> "He was a prophet and a giant among men. . . . He certainly saved the Royal Air Force from destruction in times when in any other man's hands it would have fallen".
>
> Sir Maurice Dean.

THE IMMEDIATE post-war period was one of great difficulty for the Royal Air Force, and it was in this period that Trenchard rose to his full stature in a long and sometimes bitter fight to ensure the survival of the new service. Both he and the RAF had many enemies, not least caused by the jealousy of the Army (despite the close liaison that had emerged during the War) and the Navy, both of whom wanted to see the newly created force dismembered, and the relevant parts divided between them. The RFC or RAF during a great war was one thing: a new, independent, growing force in its own right in a period of peace was another, not to be countenanced!

Trenchard was appointed Chief of the Air Staff early in 1919 by Winston Churchill, who had been appointed by Lloyd George after the 'Coupon Election' as Secretary of State for War and Air. 'You can take Air with you', Lloyd George is reputed to have said. 'I am not going to keep it as a separate department'. But Churchill had other ideas, and so did Trenchard, whom Churchill appointed as Chief of the Air Staff to replace Major-General Sir Frederick

The arrival of the airship R-34 at Mineola, Long Island, New York, on 6 July 1919, after the first direct air crossing of the Atlantic, covering 3,600 miles (5,794 km) in 108 hours 12 minutes. The R-34 was one of the most successful of all British airships.

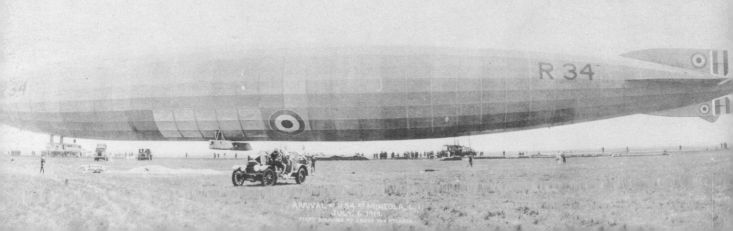

Left. *An Armstrong Whitworth Atlas picking up a message. The Atlas was designed specifically for Army co-operation and was in service through the late 1920s and well into the 1930s.*

Below. *Things did not always go well! This Handley Page Hyderabad heavy night bomber of No. 99 Squadron flipped over onto its back whilst landing. The Hyderabad entered service in 1925 and remained until 1933.*

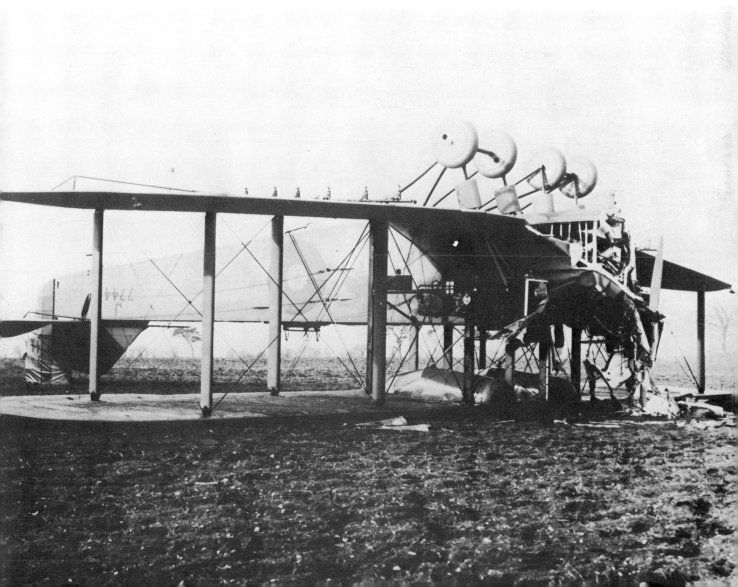

Sykes, who was made Controller of the newly-created Department of Civil Aviation.

Demobilisation was in full swing. The RAF's strength of some 280 squadrons at the end of the War was rapidly reduced to little more than one-tenth of that total, with most of the surviving units serving abroad. It has been suggested that Trenchard allowed this to happen because he wanted to rebuild the RAF from scratch in accordance with his own ideas. This is manifest nonsense. He inherited a massive, well-geared fighting machine, the finest of its kind in the world, and to try to cut it down to rebuild it in his own way would have been megalomaniacal. Rather, he fought behind the scenes vigorously to try to preserve what he could in an era of savage retrenchment. One of his greatest achievements was to ensure that the RAF was kept alive by proving its value to the country as a cheap and effective means of policing the distant parts of the Empire, including Iraq, Palestine and some of Africa.

The Government of the day was largely indifferent to the RAF. Peace had been won, bringing its own problems. No immediate enemies were looming on the horizon, so there was little need for a

The Bristol Fighter ('Brisfit'), showing pilot and rear gunner. This aircraft was one of the most formidable introduced by the RFC on the Western Front during the First World War, and it remained in service well into the post-war period.

big standing air force at home. At the same time, there was a need for economy, and aeroplanes were expensive. Although the even more difficult years of the Depression still lay ahead, the Government's bid for economies had its major impact through the Geddes Committee of 1921 – the famous 'Geddes Axe' – which virtually cut the ground from under the struggling aircraft industry, as well as cutting down the RAF.

Throughout the 1920s, there were frequent suggestions that the best economy of all would be the elimination of the RAF as a separate force, a view that had the vigorous support of some politicians, and of senior Army and Navy officers behind the scenes in Whitehall. The worst of these crises occurred in 1923, when the Admiralty claimed the return of naval aviation to the Navy. Beatty, the First Sea Lord, even threatened to resign. The Government took fright, and set up a new committee under Lord Salisbury to study the matter. A sub-committee, which included Sir William Weir, Lord Balfour and Lord Peel (Secretary for India), decided however not to hive off the naval element, and this was accepted by the main committee. The RAF survived complete.

A Hawker Horsley dropping a torpedo. The aircraft was used both as a day-bomber and a torpedo-bomber, both at home and overseas.

But in 1924 the Fleet Air Arm, comprising RAF units normally embarked on aircraft carriers and other fighting ships, came into being. This was an effective solution.

Behind the scenes, Trenchard had worked in a Herculean fashion to save the RAF from near extinction. He had by now become utterly convinced of the need for the RAF, and in the decade that he served as Chief of the Air Staff he fought many battles to keep it alive. He was not always right, but his massive strength of will, coupled with his innate vision of what the RAF could and should do for the country, ensured that when the time came, Britain still possessed a vigorous air arm (although under-equipped) staffed by a dedicated body of men and women who respected their Chief, although many also feared him.

Before Trenchard, there had been many – both politicians and serving officers – who had rendered great services to the RAF and its predecessors, the RFC and the RNAS. These included Henderson, who built the RFC and led it with such distinction through the War; Smuts, whose plan it was to create the RAF; Sir William Weir, Secretary of State for Air in the darkest days of the War; and Sir Frederick Sykes, who has been given less credit

The Fairey Flycatcher single-seat fighter was widely used in naval aviation from 1923 to 1934, and proved highly popular with pilots for its agility.

Left. *The Vickers Vimy bomber was adapted for a variety of roles in the post-war Royal Air Force, including the training of parachutists.*

Below. *King George V and Queen Mary, during a visit to the RAF School of Photography at Farnborough in 1928.*

than he deserves for his long service and great achievements, reaching back to the very foundation of the RFC itself. Above them all, however, was Trenchard. It was he who, whilst fighting politically to keep the force alive, also devoted much thought to its development. He formulated the doctrine of offence, which remained a cardinal principle of the RAF for decades, and which had its corollary in the great strategic bomber offensive of the Second World War. Trenchard has had his critics. Indeed, no man in his position, having to fight as he did, could avoid making enemies. But it is his memory that is revered, and rightly, in the RAF today.

During those ten years from 1919 to 1929, many of today's accepted RAF institutions came into being, largely because of Trenchard's efforts. He founded the RAF Benevolent Fund in October 1919. So far as RAF establishments are concerned, he set up the RAF College at Cranwell in 1920 and the Staff College at Andover in 1922 and the Apprentices School at Halton. He created a Reserve of Air Force Officers in 1923; established Short Service Commissions in 1924; established the Auxiliary Air Force and the University Air Squadrons in 1925; and helped in the creation of the Imperial Defence College in 1927, in which year he became the first Marshal of the RAF. He created the High Speed Flight in 1926 (despite some initial doubts as to its usefulness or even its propriety); and took over control of the Observer Corps (founded in 1925) from the Army in 1929.

The list is endless. If any criticism can be offered at all, it is probably that Trenchard did not look hard enough at aircraft re-equipment, and some would claim that during this period, the

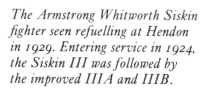

The Armstrong Whitworth Siskin fighter seen refuelling at Hendon in 1929. Entering service in 1924, the Siskin III was followed by the improved IIIA and IIIB.

The First Viscount Trenchard, Marshal of the Royal Air Force, on the left, talking to senior officers.

RAF was less well supplied with modern aircraft than it either could or should have been. But it was peacetime, with severe economic constraints at home, and time after time plans to build up the RAF from the lowest post-war level generally lapsed under pressures of limited finance. One such plan, for a front line strength of 52 squadrons, announced in 1923, to become fully effective in 1928, never even came anywhere near fruition. Financial stringency, and political indifference held it back. Depression came in 1929, and with it further cuts. It was not until the resurgence of Germany in 1933–34 that defence began to be taken at all seriously in Britain, and even then it took years of further struggle before the RAF began to expand again. Long before then, however, Trenchard had handed over the reins of office. He gave up active duty with the RAF in 1929, but his voice, though no longer as authoritative with the trappings of power, was never still, and he continued publicly and privately to advocate his policies for many years.

As the first Viscount Trenchard, he became Commissioner of the Metropolitan Police. He lived to see his policies of offensive air power vindicated during the Second World War. He died on 10 February 1956, aged 83, but his memory lives on in the great fighting force he created.

5 The RAF Overseas
1919–1939

THE RAF's involvement in overseas theatres in the period between the Wars stemmed from the RFC's own activities during the First World War. As early as July 1916 a Middle East Brigade had been formed in Egypt, under Brigadier General W. G. H. Salmond, co-ordinating RFC units in Macedonia, Mesopotamia, Palestine and East Africa under one command. The RFC had also fought extensively against the Turks. Even before the end of the war, the big Handley Page 0/400 bombers – the 'Bloody Paralysers' – had begun making long distance flights, including that from Cranwell to Cairo in July 1918.

At the end of the War, the RAF set up the 86th (Communications) Wing at Hendon to provide rapid transport between London and Paris to serve with the Peace Conference, the first regular air service between those two cities. Also in December 1918 the first England–India flight was made by a Handley Page V/1500 bomber, the 'Old Carthusian', leaving Martlesham on 13 December and arriving at Karachi on 30 December. The RAF also controlled the newly-created Department of Civil Aviation, set up in January 1919, under Sir Frederick Sykes.

In the same year, British and world enthusiasm for aviation was stirred again by the epic transatlantic non-stop flight from St Johns, Newfoundland, to Clifden, Ireland, on 14 and 15 June by Captain John Alcock and Lieutenant Arthur Whitten Brown in a modified Vickers Vimy bomber, making the 1,890 miles (3,042 km) crossing in 16 hours 27 minutes airborne. Both were knighted for their achievements.

Trenchard's own ideas for the survival of the RAF included a substantial measure of overseas operations. His plan for the peace-time air force, put forward in December 1919, included provision for eight squadrons and one depot in India, seven squadrons and one depot in Egypt; three squadrons and one depot in Mesopotamia; one seaplane flight in Malta; one seaplane flight in

Opposite. The Vickers Victoria Mark IV troop-carriers of No. 216 Squadron, seen in formation over the Pyramids during the Silver Jubilee celebrations in Cairo, in 1935.

Right. *The Vickers Victoria troop-carrier entered service in 1926 in Iraq and Egypt, and saw extensive service elsewhere overseas, performing many notable flights, including the famous evacuation from Kabul in late 1928-early 1929.*

Below. *Fairey IIIFs of No. 47 Squadron at Khartoum in 1930. This two-seat day bomber and general purpose aircraft made many of the RAF's pioneering long-distance flights.*

The RAF base at Heliopolis, Egypt, in 1929. This was one of the RAF's key overseas bases both in its Empire 'policing' role of the inter-war years, and during the Second World War.

Alexandria; and one seaplane flight on a carrier in the Mediter-ranean. All were to be very active, and capable of reinforcement from home in the event of trouble. Trenchard's objective was to demonstrate to the politicians at home that the air arm could be used swiftly and more cheaply than any other military force to ensure the peace in, and keep control of, the UK's many wide-spread possessions overseas. It worked. The RAF's first 'little war' overseas was in joint operations with the Camel Corps in Somali-land in 1920, when RAF units were the main instrument and decisive factor in the overthrow of the 'Mad Mullah' in an offensive lasting three weeks, after he had defied British military power since 1900.

In June 1921, the RAF began the weekly mail service between Cairo and Baghdad, after the 840 mile (1,352 km) route had been surveyed and tracks ploughed by motor vehicles across the Syrian desert to assist navigation. The service was operated by the RAF until early in 1927, when it was taken over by the newly-formed Imperial Airways. The Military Control of Iraq was handed over to the RAF in 1922. The Palestine Command was formed in 1924; while in October 1925, the RAF checked outrages by the Mahsud tribes in Waziristan by bombing their villages after the inhabitants had been evacuated. In the following year, the RAF again pioneered what was to become a vital civil air route, with the first flight from Cairo to the Cape and back, by four Fairey IIIDs. Leaving on 1 March they returned to Cairo on 27 May, when they were equipped with floats and flown to England, arriving on 21 June at Lee-on-Solent, having completed a 14,000 mile (22,531 km) cruise.

In 1927, the RAF had set up its China headquarters in Hong Kong, while a fleet of four Southampton flying boats made the first Far East flight, leaving Felixstowe on 14 October, and then Plymouth on 17 October, for a 27,000 mile (43,452 km) cruise, taking in Egypt, India, Australia, Hong Kong and Singapore.

The defence of Aden and its surrounding territory was taken over by the RAF early in 1928. In Afghanistan, the RAF aided in the evacuation of 586 civilians from Kabul following the isolation of the British Legation there by rebel tribes led by Kabibullah Khan. This was an epic RAF achievement, for it involved flying in Vickers Victoria transports some 28,160 miles (45,319 km) in all, including flying at about 10,000 feet (3,048 metres) over mountains in severe winter weather. This varied type of operation continued through the ensuing years, with the RAF not only undertaking punitive military operations against defecting tribes in various parts of the Middle East, Africa and elsewhere, but also pioneering what were to become eventually some of the world's major air routes, and undertaking some epic long-distance flights.

These included setting up a World Distance Record in

Opposite. *Supermarine Southampton flying-boats at Hinaidi in 1927. The Southamptons were used extensively by the RAF for long-distance pioneering flights, including that to Egypt, India, Australia, Hong Kong and Singapore in 1927.*

In addition to policing duties
overseas, the RAF performed
many other roles, including the
provision of 'air ambulance'
services. A DH-9 is shown in
this role in Somaliland in 1919.

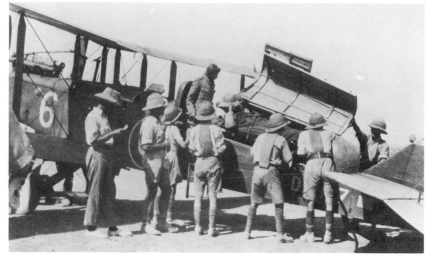

A Vickers Vernon loading a
stretcher-case during operations in
Iraq.

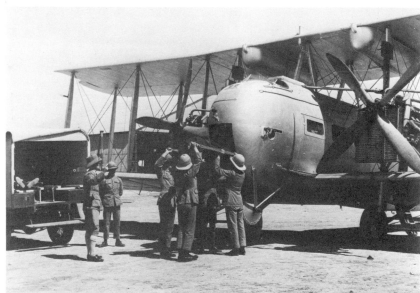

The inspection of men of No. 70
Squadron on the successful
completion of the evacuation of
586 civilians from Kabul,
Afghanistan, after the revolt by
tribes led by Kabibullah Khan.
The operation, in severe winter
weather over the mountains, began
in December 1928, and was
completed the following February.

February 1933 from Cranwell to Walvis Bay, South Africa, in a Fairey Long-Range Monoplane, a distance of 5,309 miles (8,544 km) in 57 hours 25 minutes, by Squadron Leader O. R. Gayford and Flight Lieutenant G. E. Nicholetts.

The RAF's Long Range Development Flight also subsequently set up a new World Distance Record when two Vickers Wellesley bombers flew from Ismailia, Egypt, to Darwin, Australia on 5 to 7 November 1938, a distance of 7,162 miles (11,526 km) in 48 hours, with a third Wellesley reaching Koepang in the Netherlands East Indies. This was the last of the many great pioneering flights by the RAF, however, for by that time rearmament was in full spate again to prepare for the war that everyone in the RAF realised was on the way. There was no longer time for epic journeys. Every effort was being put into strengthening the RAF.

Throughout the twenty years from 1919 to 1939 there can be no doubt that the overseas activities of the RAF, often working under acute difficulties and economic constraints, and by Herculean efforts, achieved three things. First, the RAF gave Britain the effective and consistent control of many of its overseas territories for a comparatively miniscule sum. Secondly, it helped in the creation of an Empire air service, ultimately operated by Imperial Airways, that was second to none anywhere in the world. Lastly, it helped to keep alive in British minds that enthusiasm for aviation that was, as Trenchard had clearly seen, so desperately necessary a factor in the overall survival of the RAF.

It was not always a success story, however. The Government and the RAF had retained an interest in airship development, culminating in the R-101 of 1930. This was intended to be one of the great passenger craft for long distance air travel and its maiden voyage to India in early October was widely publicised in advance,

Fairey IIIFs of No. 202 Squadron, at Khartoum in 1934. These aircraft were used for a wide range of tasks, including communications and reconnaissance, and for long-distance flying.

Right. *This incident occurred in Baghdad in 1921 when a Bristol Fighter of No. 30 Squadron (Army Co-operation) took off with a mechanic sitting astride the rear fuselage.*

Below. *Westland Wapitis at Gilgit, in Kashmir. The Wapiti day-bomber was widely used by the RAF at home and overseas in general purpose and reconnaissance as well as bomber roles. They escorted the Victorias in the famous evacuation from Kabul in late 1928-early 1929.*

but proved to be an utter disaster (the private venture R-100 was much more successful). The R-101 crashed in a storm near Beauvais, France, on 5 October, killing the Air Minister, Lord Thomson of Cardington, and many other dignitaries, with only six survivors out of 54 on board. The result was that the Government and the RAF abandoned airship development, and to this day there has been little British military interest in airships beyond the use of barrage balloons.

Nevertheless, throughout the period between the wars, public opinion was on the side of the RAF, despite what the politicians might want to do to the service. That opinion was of cardinal importance to the RAF both then, in helping Trenchard to keep the politicians at bay, and also in the struggles that were to follow. It was because of the RAF's successes overseas that enthusiasm to join the service remained high, so that when the call came in the late 1930s for recruits for the by-then rapidly expanding service, there was no lack of willing young men whose excitement for aviation had been kindled and sustained by the stirring exploits of the immediate past.

Fairey IIIFs of No. 8 Squadron, over Bir Ali, Aden, in 1934.

6 The Schneider Trophy Races
1927–1931

"Frankly, I am against this contest. . . . I can see nothing of value in it."
Lord Trenchard, to the Secretary of State for Air.

IN ADDITION TO the pioneering long-distance flights made in the period between the wars, the RAF also pushed the frontiers of flying higher and higher and faster and faster. In September 1936 Squadron Leader F. R. D. Swain, flying the new Bristol 138A research aircraft from Farnborough, climbed to a height of just over 49,900 feet (15,209.5 metres), setting a new World Altitude Record. On 30 June 1937, this was beaten by Flight Lieutenant M. J. Adam, also flying an improved version of the Bristol 138A, who climbed to 53,937 feet (16,440 metres), also from Farnborough.

Of all the events which stirred the hearts and minds of the British public in favour of aviation during the inter-war years, none matched the Schneider Trophy Races. This great series of international competitions for seaplanes, flown annually (apart from occasional cancellations) throughout the 1920s, and biennially from 1927 to 1931, captured public imagination world-wide, but nowhere so much as in Britain and Italy, the two greatest protagonists. The races had been initiated before the First World War by a Frenchman, Jacques Schneider, who saw in the idea the possibilities of developing seaplanes for peaceful purposes, including commerce. His dream prevailed until the early 1920s, when it was progressively taken over and adapted by others, acquiring nationalistic overtones. The Races became eventually the open arena for competition between the air forces of several nations, notably Britain and Italy, as well as a means of forcing the pace of development of airframes and engines. But the Races also helped to generate that national mood in favour of aviation, and military aviation in particular, that was to be of such great value to the RAF at a time of acute economic depression and financial stringency.

The progressive development of the Supermarine high-speed aircraft, which eventually won the Schneider Trophy outright for Britain in 1931, is shown in this series of pictures.

The top picture shows the S-5, which won the race at Venice on 26 September 1927, flown by Flight Lieutenant S. N. Webster, of the RAF's High Speed Flight.

In the centre is the improved S-6, in which Flying Officer H. R. D. Waghorn won the 1929 race on 7 September at Calshot.

At the bottom is the S-6B in which Flight Lieutenant J. N. Boothman won the race at Calshot (Spithead) on 13 September 1931, thereby securing three victories in a row for Britain and effectively ending the Series.

The architects of victory, both in the Schneider Trophy Races and eventually also the Battle of Britain. Reginald J. Mitchell, the designer from Supermarine, on the left, with Henry Royce (later Sir Henry), in 1929. From their work on the Schneider Trophy Races eventually emerged the matchless combination of Spitfire and Merlin engine, which played so significant a role in the Battle of Britain. Unfortunately, neither lived to see it, as Royce died in 1933 and Mitchell, in 1936.

The Races had been initiated by Schneider in December 1912 with the first event actually taking place at Monaco in 1913, when it was won by Maurice Prévost of France, flying a Deperdussin with an average speed of 45.75 mph (73.62 km/h). Again at Monaco, in 1914, Howard Pixton won the race for Britain, flying a Sopwith Tabloid at 86.78 mph (139.66 km/h). Then the First World War intervened, and the third race was not held until September 1919, at Bournemouth Bay. On that occasion, the Italians were believed by many to have won, but were robbed of the prize by a disqualification. Subsequently, the Italians won both races at Venice in 1920 and 1921, pushing the average speed up first to 107.22 mph (172.55 km/h) and then to 117.9 mph (189.74 km/h). Because the rules laid down that any country, club, organisation or individual, who won the race three times in five years could hold it in perpetuity, the Italians felt they had been robbed of the trophy as a result of their disqualification in 1919.

The rules were upheld, however, and it was still open for Britain to win again. This happened at Naples, in 1922, when Henri Biard, the chief test pilot of Supermarine, won the race with an average of 145.7 mph (234.48 km/h) in a Supermarine Sea Lion II with a 450 hp Napier Lion engine. It was around this time that the genius of a young designer, Reginald Mitchell, who had joined

Supermarine as a draughtsman in 1916, and who master-minded the development of the Sea Lion II from an early design of seaplane hull, began to make his presence felt.

The Americans, represented by a US naval team, won in 1923 at Cowes, but the race planned for Baltimore in 1924 was cancelled because Italy withdrew and Britain's entry, the Gloster II, had crashed during trials. The Americans won again in 1925, also at Baltimore, but the Italians came back hard to win – on Mussolini's direct order – at Hampton Roads in 1926.

It was at this stage that the RAF came into the picture. The Air Ministry had been studying ideas for high-speed seaplanes for some time, and on 1 October 1926, a High Speed Flight was set up at Felixstowe, to test the new aircraft, and fly in the race. This decision had not been achieved without some considerable heart-searching inside the Air Ministry. Some senior officers, such as Geoffrey Salmond, were much in favour, but Trenchard himself was dubious. He complained that the Royal Aero Club had given him inaccurate information about the Schneider Trophy Races, but after a period of disquiet, and still nursing doubts, he finally agreed to RAF participation. The Treasury (then headed by Winston Churchill) had to be persuaded, however. The Air Council, once Trenchard had approved, argued powerfully that the building and flying of high-speed aircraft would be valuable both for the RAF as well as the aircraft industry. Since 1923, all the successful teams in

The Supermarine S-6 (N247), in which Flying Officer H. R. D. Waghorn won the 1929 contest at Calshot, seen being secured to its landing lighter in the Solent.

The Schneider Trophy victories could never have been achieved without the intensive work undertaken by Rolls-Royce on the 'R' engine. It is seen here on the test-bed at Derby in 1931, surrounded by the engineering team involved. On the right is Francis ('Rod') Banks, the oil expert who evolved the special 'fuel cocktail' which enabled the engine to achieve the sustained power necessary for victory.

the Races had been military teams, and if Britain was to win at all, it would have to be with a service entry.

The Air Ministry's pressure was successful. The Treasury agreed, and preparations for the race went ahead. It took place at Venice, on 26 September, when Flight Lieutenant Sidney N. Webster, flying a Supermarine S-5, designed by R. J. Mitchell, with an 875 hp Napier Lion engine, won with an average speed of 281.65 mph (453.27 km/h). Second was Flight Lieutenant O. E. Worsley, also flying an S-5, with an average speed of 273.07 mph (439.46 km/h). Another member of the High Speed Flight, Flight Lieutenant S. M. Kinkead, came fourth, in a Gloster IVB, even though he had been obliged to retire after completing only five of the seven laps of 50 kilometres each.

The RAF was jubilant, but Trenchard's old objections returned when the question arose of participating in the 1929 race (which under the rules was due to be held at Calshot, near Spithead). He felt that it was to the detriment of the RAF that it should be used to win public air races, and that although such events might be of benefit to the aircraft industry, they did not necessarily teach the bulk of the RAF very much. But Trenchard was overruled. The Cabinet liked the idea of a British attempt to retain the Trophy, and early in 1928 the Air Ministry was given the go-ahead to make its

Another view of the Rolls-Royce 'R' engine on the test-bed at Derby. With intensive effort, the engine was developed very quickly from an existing engine, the Buzzard. It was progressively uprated from 1,900 hp to an eventual 2,550 hp, thus enabling the High Speed Flight not only to win the Trophy outright, on 13 September 1931, but also to set a new World Absolute Speed record of 407.5 mph (655.81 km/h), on 29 September 1931.

preparations. R. J. Mitchell of Supermarine wanted a bigger engine for his revamped Supermarine S-6, and Rolls-Royce was asked to produce it. Henry Royce (later knighted for his efforts) and his team took an existing engine, the Buzzard, and turned it quickly into the new 'R' engine, of 1,900 hp, in a period of astonishingly intensive activity.

The RAF won the Race on 7 September at Calshot, when Flying Officer H. R. D. Waghorn of the High Speed Flight, flying the Supermarine S-6, achieved an average speed of 328.63 mph (528.88 km/h). On 7 September Flight Lieutenant R. L. R. Atcherley established a 100 km closed circuit speed record of 331.32 mph (533.21 km/h), also in the S-6, while a few days later, on 12 September, another member of the High Speed Flight, Squadron Leader A. H. Orlebar gave the RAF a triple triumph by setting up a World Absolute Speed Record in the S-6 of 357.75 mph (575.74 km/h).

The Race came round again in 1931, and Britain had the chance to seize the Trophy outright. But the Government this time demurred. It was the time of the Depression, strict economy was being enforced, and there was no money in the kitty for such frivolities as air races. But the Cabinet finally decided, in response to aircraft industry and public pressures, that if the Royal Aero Club could find a sponsor, it would authorise the Air Ministry to

The indomitable Lady Lucy Houston, whose benefaction of £100,000 enabled the 1931 race to take place. She is seen at Calshot, accompanied by delighted RAF Officers.

enter an RAF team. It was at this stage that the Royal Aero Club discovered a Fairy Godmother, in the person of Lady Lucy Houston, the widow of a shipping magnate. She offered to put up £100,000 of her own money for the Race, rumbustiously castigating the Government for its parsimony. She declared firmly that:

> When the Socialist Government gave the paltry excuse that they could not afford the expenses necessary for England's airmen to participate in the race for the Schneider Trophy, my blood boiled with indignation, for I know that every true Briton would rather sell his last shirt than admit that England could not afford to defend herself before all comers.

The Race was thus held on 13 September at Spithead, again with the participation of the RAF High Speed Flight, using a new version of the Supermarine, the S-6B, also designed by Mitchell, and a new version of the 'R' engine of 2,350 hp. Piloted by Flight Lieutenant J. N. Boothman, this aircraft won the Trophy outright for Britain with no challengers with an average speed of 340.08 mph (547.30 km/h). On the same day, Flight Lieutenant G. H. Stain-

forth, also of the High Speed Flight, used the S-6B to put the World Absolute Speed Record up to 379.05 mph (610.02 km/h). Two weeks later, on 29 September, with the 'R' engine further boosted to 2,550 hp, he put the record up again to 407.5 mph (655.81 km/h).

The Schneider Trophy belonged to Britain outright, and the RAF was toasted world-wide. Whether the RAF itself gained any immediate technological benefit from its victories is debatable. What it undeniably did gain, however, was enormous prestige and credibility throughout the world, and especially at home. The aircraft industry gained equally from the massive advances in airframe and engine design that the Schneider Trophy Races induced. For from the work done in the previous four years, there was to emerge in the early 1930s a new airframe and engine combination, from the Supermarine stable run by R. J. Mitchell and from Rolls-Royce: the Spitfire and the Merlin. It is not going too far to say that, had the RAF not participated in the Schneider Trophy Races of 1927–31, there might never have emerged – at least not in sufficient time – that matchless combination which in the hands of the RAF saved Britain in the great Battle in 1940.

The winning Schneider Trophy team from the RAF High Speed Flight in 1931, in front of the S-6B in which Flight Lieutenant G. H. Stainforth, set the World Absolute Speed Record on 13 September at 379.05 mph (610.02 km/h) and raised it again on 29 September to 407.5 mph (655.81 km/h).

The team, left to right, were: Flight Lieutenant E. J. L. Hope, Lieutenant R. L. Brinton, who died before the Race, Flight Lieutenant F. W. Long, Flight Lieutenant G. H. Stainforth, Squadron Leader A. H. Orlebar, Flight Lieutenant J. N. Boothman, Flying Officer L. S. Snaith and Flight Lieutenant W. Dry.

7 The Build-up to War

1931–1939

"The only real security upon which sound military principles will rely is that you should be master of your own air."

Winston Churchill

THE 1930s were a period of increasing turbulence in European political affairs, during which time it became increasingly apparent that rearmament was essential, even long overdue, and that the strength of the Royal Air Force desperately needed increasing. But the expansion came slowly.

Even as late as 1934, the year after Adolf Hitler had come to power in Germany, there was still uncertainty about what should be done. The Prime Minister (Stanley Baldwin) told the House of Commons in that year that if the International Disarmament Conference failed, steps would be taken to bring about an Air Disarmament Conference: if that failed in turn, the Government would start to bring the RAF strength up to that of the strongest air force within striking distance of the UK. The Conference attempts did fail, and in July 1934, the first of many schemes to increase the RAF was put forward, envisaging a rise in the strength of the Home Defence force from 52 to 75 squadrons, with other additions, spread over five years. The aim was to provide a total first-line strength of 128 squadrons in that time-scale.

The political situation deteriorated progressively. In October 1935, Italy invaded, and eventually conquered, Abyssinia (Ethiopia). In March 1936, Hitler's forces moved into the Rhineland, in violation of the Treaty of Versailles. Later in 1936, civil war broke out in Spain. Germany and Italy supported the Franco regime, mainly with air power, and that gave those two countries' air forces much experience that was to prove invaluable training for the assaults that were to come later in Holland, Belgium and France.

In March 1938, Hitler annexed Austria, a move also forbidden by the Treaty of Versailles, and by now it was clear that war in Europe could be avoided only by a miracle. The British Prime Minister, Neville Chamberlain, tried to stop Hitler's onward march, now directed against Czechoslovakia, by negotiation. His efforts were an abysmal failure.

While all this was going on, efforts to expand the RAF were still being pursued in Whitehall. Various schemes for such expansion were put forward, but initially it seemed that Britain was not yet prepared to pay the necessary price for an adequate air arm, despite warnings by Winston Churchill that the German air force was rapidly approaching parity with that of Britain. It was not until the Defence White Paper of 1936 that a serious scheme to provide up to 124 squadrons for the Home Defence Force was put forward, to be completed by March 1939. This scheme also included plans for the provision of a full scale of reserves (the RAF Volunteer Reserve), and first steps were taken towards the provision of 'shadow' factories for the production of aircraft.

The Hendon Air Displays of the 1930s did much to stimulate public interest in the RAF and in aviation generally. The picture shows the 1931 Display, including the New Types Park with the experimental Westland–Hill Pterodactyl tail-less fighter, which was never developed.

Right. *The versatile Hawker Hart light bomber entered service in January 1930. About 460 were eventually built by Hawker, Armstrong Whitworth, Vickers and Gloster Aircraft. The Hart remained in service until it was superseded by the Hind and the Blenheim.*

Opposite. *Arming a Gloster Gladiator. The last of the RAF's biplane fighters, it went into service in 1937.*

The RAF airfield at Northolt in 1931. This station is one of the oldest RAF flying establishments – it is still in service today, primarily as a communications base serving London.

Right. *The Bristol Bulldog was one of the most famous of the RAF's fighters and trainers between the wars, with over 300 built. They performed regularly at the highly popular public air displays at Hendon in the 1930s.*

Below. *The aircraft service park at Hendon, in June 1932, showing many of the types of aircraft in service at the time, including Boulton & Paul Overstrands, Hawker Hinds, Hawker Furies, Bristol Bulldogs, Avro 504s and de Havilland DH-9s.*

Left. *Bristol Blenheim Is of No. 30 Squadron over Lake Habaniya in September 1938. The Blenheim bomber was one of the first new aircraft to emerge under the RAF's Expansion Scheme in the build-up to war.*

Below. *The Hawker Fury has been described as the most elegant of all the RAF's biplane fighters, and was the standard interceptor through the 1930s, eventually being superseded by the Hurricane.*

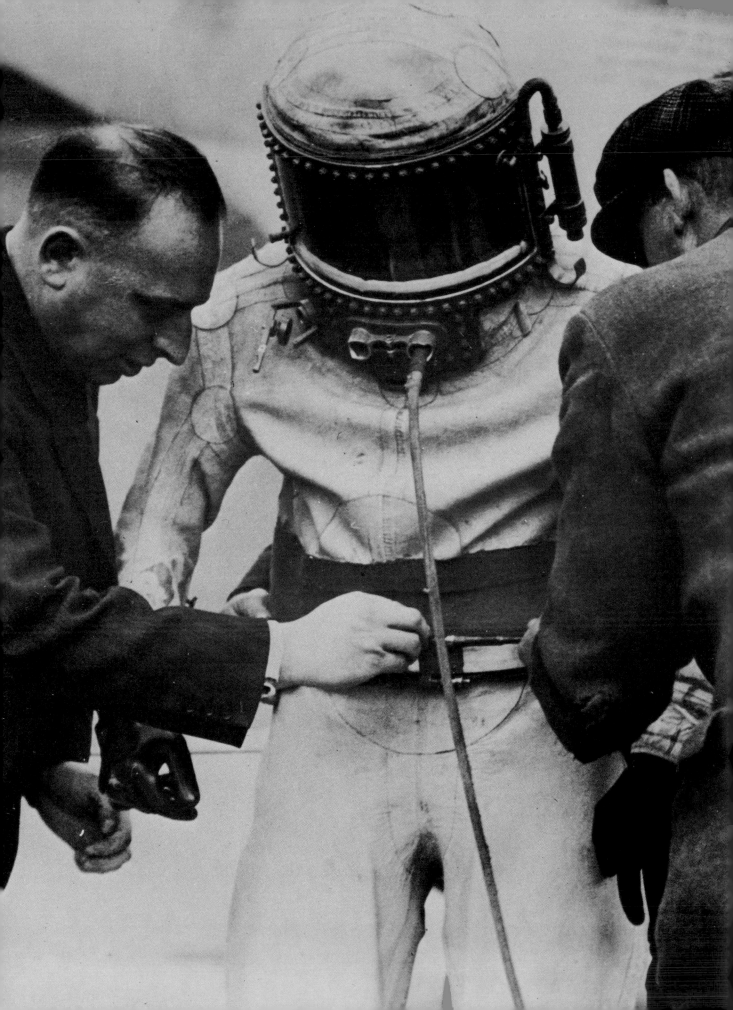

Schemes for further expansion were put forward later to Prime Minister Neville Chamberlain, but not adopted. It was not until after the Munich crisis in September 1938, when Britain came almost to the brink of war with Germany, that a much bigger programme of expansion was adopted, with the emphasis on fighters and heavy bombers, and by February 1939, the Cabinet, now well aware that war was only months away, authorised the greatest production of aircraft possible.

The effect of these late decisions is seen in the fact that whereas in 1938, Britain's aircraft production amounted to only 2,827 compared with Germany's 5,235, by 1939 it had reached 7,940, still behind Germany's 8,295, but improving rapidly. The build-up between 1938 and 1939 was concentrated on Fighter Command. In July 1936 the Home Defence (Air Defence of Great Britain) was reorganised into four Commands. Bomber Command was under Air Chief Marshal Sir John Steel; Fighter Command, under Air Marshal Sir Hugh Dowding; Coastal under Air Marshal Sir Arthur Longmore; and Training, under Air Marshal Sir Charles Burnett. The formation of Maintenance, Balloon and Reserve Commands came later. The Women's Auxiliary Air Force was formed in 1939.

The RAF's first eight-gun fighter, the Hurricane, designed

Opposite. The pressure suit specially developed by the Royal Aircraft Establishment, Farnborough, for the RAF's successful bids to set new World Altitude Records in the Bristol 138A in 1936 and again in 1937.

Westland Wallaces of No. 501 Squadron of the Auxiliary Air Force. The Wallace was developed from the Wapiti in 1931 as a general purpose biplane. In all, 172 were built.

and built originally as a private venture by Hawker to the design by Sydney Camm, entered service in December 1937, with No. 111 Squadron at Northolt. The Supermarine Spitfire, designed by R. J. Mitchell's team, entered service in June 1938, with No. 19 Squadron at Duxford.

Re-equipment had been left so late, however, and the RAF had so few aircraft, that in June 1938, it was announced that Britain was to buy 200 Lockheed Hudsons and 200 North American Harvards from the US.

The strength of public concern by this time at the need for readiness against the onset of war is illustrated by the fact that on 20 May 1939, the last of the great Empire Air Days held between the wars to highlight British air power, saw more than one million people crowding into 60 RAF stations and 18 other airfields that were opened to the public.

It has been argued that the year after the Munich crisis bought Britain valuable time in its belated rearmament programme, and that had war come in the autumn of 1938, Britain would have been far from prepared. This is probably true, for in 1938, the re-equipment of Fighter Command with Hurricanes and Spitfires was only just beginning. By 1 January 1939 RAF strength comprised 135 squadrons: 74 of bombers, 27 of fighters, 12 for Army co-operation, 17 for reconnaissance, four for torpedo bombing and one for communications. The Auxiliary Air Force strength comprised 19 squadrons: three bomber, 11 fighter, two for Army co-operation and three reconnaissance. A year later, there were still only 35 squadrons in Fighter Command, of which 26 were equipped with Hurricanes and Spitfires. In bombers, the Fairey Battle (1936) and

The DH-82 Tiger Moth was the RAF's elementary trainer for more than 15 years. It first entered service in February 1932, and was still being used as late as 1951 with the RAF Volunteer Reserve. Thousands of RAF pilots learned to fly on this most forgiving of aeroplanes.

Left. *Mr. (later Sir) Sydney Camm, one of this country's greatest aircraft designers, was responsible for a long line of aircraft, but particularly the Hawker Hurricane fighter.*

Below. *Hawker Hurricanes in production during the Second World War. In all, 12,780 were built in Britain (mostly by Hawker, but including 2,750 by Gloster), with another 1,451 built in Canada, by the Canadian Car and Foundry Company.*

Right. *The Supermarine Spitfire prototype made its maiden flight from the company's Eastleigh, Southampton, airfield on 5 March 1936. This legendary combination of R. J. Mitchell's aeronautical genius and the Rolls-Royce Merlin engine, is probably the most famous fighter of all time, with 20,351 having been built in various versions (including those powered by Rolls-Royce Griffon engines, but excluding the Seafire version).*

Below. *The Short Sarafand six-engined flying-boat (with Rolls-Royce Buzzard engines) was an experimental aircraft, sponsored by Lord Trenchard shortly before he left the RAF. Only one aircraft was built, flying first on 30 June 1932.*

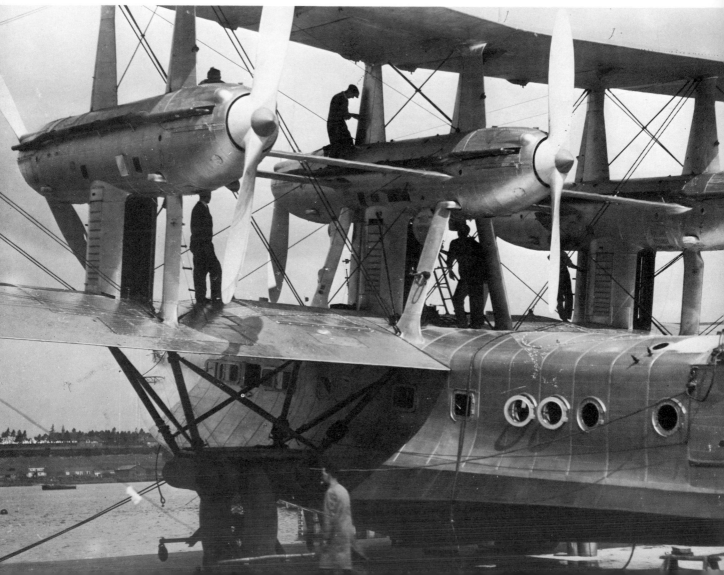

the Bristol Blenheim were moving into squadron service, followed by the Armstrong Whitworth Whitley (1937), the Handley Page Hampden and Vickers Wellington (1938). The Hurricanes and Spitfires were to carry the burden of the great aerial battles in the first year of the war. The bomber types were to be the mainstay of Bomber Command until the new generation of four-engined Halifaxes, Stirlings and twin-engined Manchesters (later to be developed into the four Merlin-engined Lancaster) began to enter service. The Sunderland flying-boat, which was to perform such valuable service in the bitter anti-submarine warfare that lay ahead, entered service with Coastal Command in 1938.

The scope of this build-up of the RAF can be gauged from the money being spent on it. From as little as £9.4m. in March 1934, the figure rose to £18.6m. in 1936, doubled to £39.3m. in 1937, nearly doubled again to £66m. in 1938, and by 1939 had reached the (for then) astronomical sum of nearly £110m. – although of course during the war years it was to go much higher still.

By the outbreak of war in September 1939, the RAF had an actual front-line strength of 1,911 aircraft, with another 1,600

The de Havilland Dominie was the military version of the well-known Rapide light airliner. It was widely used in the 1930s and during the Second World War for training and communications duties. Over 500 were built, including a number for the Fleet Air Arm.

The Hawker Hurricane was one of the most famous fighters of the RAF, sharing with the Spitfire the credit for the victory in the Battle of Britain in 1940, and serving in many overseas theatres. In all, 12,780 Hurricanes of various versions were built in Britain, and another 1,451 were built in Canada.

The Armstrong Whitworth Whitley twin-engined bomber prototype first flew on 17 March 1936. It was intended as a long-range night bomber, and entered service with No. 10 Squadron at Dishforth, Yorkshire, in March 1937.

described as 'serviceable first-line aircraft', and another 2,200 aircraft in reserve. By comparison, Germany had 3,609 front-line aircraft, 2,893 'serviceable first-line aircraft' and some 900 in reserve. Britain was still building up her air force fast, however. Production of 7,940 aircraft in 1939 soared to reach 15,049 in 1940, outstripping that of Germany (10,826). It went higher still thereafter, reaching a peak of over 26,000 in 1943 and 1944 – although in those years, despite the bombing offensive, Germany was also to achieve miracles of aircraft production, reaching over 25,000 in 1943 and an incredible 39,000 in 1944.

By the time of General Mobilisation of the RAF on 24 August 1939, the battle lines had been broadly set, and an air of expectancy gripped the Service.

The Battle of Britain and 'The Few'

1940

8

"Never in the field of human conflict was so much owed by so many to so few".

Winston Churchill.

ON 2 SEPTEMBER, the day before war was declared, and just after the German attack on Poland, the first twelve squadrons of the Advanced Air Striking Force (ten of Battles and two of Hurricanes) flew to France. They were accompanied by the Air Component of the British Expeditionary Force, comprising four squadrons of Lysanders, four of Blenheims and four of Hurricanes and Gladiators.

War on Germany was declared on 3 September, but for a few months, although the RAF squadrons based at home were busy with photographic reconnaissance, leaflet raids over Hamburg, Bremen and the Ruhr, and with attacks on German shipping in harbour, and on U-boats at sea, there was little in the way of major aerial fighting.

Those few months were invaluable, however, in that they enabled the RAF to continue its build-up, with increasing deliveries of Spitfires and Hurricanes, and further training of pilots and ground crews. Just as significantly, work continued with the perfecting of the operational use of the secret RDF (Radio Direction Finding: the name Radar was coined later) network that had been built up in the late 1930s and that was to serve Fighter Command well when the great air battle began in the summer of 1940.

During this period also, a major step forward was taken with the introduction of the Empire Air Training Scheme, that was to be so valuable throughout the War in training many thousands of pilots and other aircrew, especially for Bomber Command, in Canada, Australia and New Zealand, South Africa and Southern Rhodesia.

One especially significant development in the summer of 1940

Right. *The Supermarine Spitfire saw action in many war theatres, especially overseas, where it was popular with its pilots for its smooth handling and superb performance.*

Below. *The recruit gets his first glimpse of the RAF depot. With other volunteers he enters the depot for examination.*

was the complete reorganisation of aircraft production, following the 14 May appointment by Prime Minister Winston Churchill of Lord Beaverbrook as the Minister for Aircraft Production. Although Beaverbrook's abrasive methods were much criticised, he galvanised the aircraft industry. As a result they were able to provide the necessary fighter replenishments that proved so valuable as the forces built up over the preceding three years were whittled down as the great Battle of Britain raged throughout the summer of 1940.

Prior to the Battle of Britain itself, the RAF played a major role first in the Battle of Norway, and then later in the Battle of France, as the German armies swept through the Low Countries and into France itself. The RAF Component of the British Expeditionary Force together with the Advanced Air Striking Force was small, but they played a major role in harassing the advancing German armies and incurred heavy losses. By the time the Air Component was withdrawn to Britain, when it became clear that defeat in France was inevitable, the original force of over 260 aircraft had been reduced to only 65. Additional squadrons of Hurricanes had been sent to France in early May, and by the middle of that month some 22 squadrons of Hurricanes were committed,

A familiar scene at airfields in Southern England during the Battle of Britain in the late summer of 1940 – a Spitfire being re-armed between sorties.

The Boulton Paul Defiant two-seat turret fighter entered service late in 1939, initially as a day fighter, but subsequently as a night fighter, when it was found that it was no match for enemy single-seaters. Nevertheless, over 1,000 were built before production ceased in early 1943.

The Fairey Battle three-seat light bomber saw much active service in the first year of the war, but although manned by gallant and courageous crews, it proved underpowered and was out-fought by enemy aircraft. It was withdrawn from front-line service and relegated to the training role in late 1940.

The Hawker Hurricane, which sprang from the design genius of Sydney Camm, was built in many versions. Shown here is an early variant on a test flight. The aircraft was powered by the Rolls-Royce Merlin engine.

dangerously whittling down the number of squadrons at home. Efforts by the French Government to get more squadrons were resisted by the Chiefs of Staff, primarily because of the need to retain them for the defence of the UK.

The RAF contingent in France was thus withdrawn, and it was from their bases at home that Fighter Command flew more than 2,700 sorties to cover the evacuation of the British Army from the beaches of Dunkirk in late May and early June. The air superiority established over the beaches was the key to the success of that evacuation. Had there not been such cover, the British Army would have been utterly destroyed, where it lay, virtually helpless on the sea-shore and awaiting rescue.

The Battle of Britain is officially regarded as having commenced on 10 July 1940. By that time the remnants of the British Army had been rescued from the beaches of Dunkirk and the

Sqn. Ldr. Robert Stanford Tuck DSO, DFC and bar, in command of No. 257 Squadron which had been adopted by Burma. The Burmese flag is painted on the aircraft.

RAF Middle Wallop members of No. 609 Squadron just after a bombing raid in August 1940.

German conquest of the Low Countries and France had been completed. The Luftwaffe was able to move its forward units close to the coast of occupied Europe, giving the shortest possible flight times across the English Channel.

When the Battle began in July, Fighter Command, under Air Chief Marshal Sir Hugh Dowding, had an average daily operational force of some 600–700 fighters, mostly Hurricanes and Spitfires, pitted against an operational Luftwaffe strength of about 1,000 fighters and 1,250 bombers. The German bombers were mostly Heinkel 111s, Dornier 17s and Junkers 87s and 88s. The Battle was one of fighter against fighter initially, with the British and German aircraft evenly matched, the Messerschmidt had an advantage in climb, against the Spitfire's manoeuvrability.

The Battle was fought in five phases. The first, or preliminary, phase from 10 July to 7 August, was devoted to Luftwaffe attacks on British shipping in the Channel, in a bid to cut supply lines but also to try to draw out and destroy Britain's fighter forces. The next two phases are generally considered to be the most critical periods. From 8 to 18 August, along with continued attacks on shipping and coastal towns, the basic enemy objective was to destroy Fighter Command on the ground and in the air; and from 19 August to 6 September, there were even stronger direct attacks on Fighter

Command's airfields, in a bid to destroy the bases from which the RAF operated.

By 6 September, it was clear that the Luftwaffe had failed to achieve its first priority – the destruction of Fighter Command in the air, so that in the fourth phase of the Battle, from 7 September to 5 October, the enemy switched the main attacks to daylight raids on London and other cities. The effect of Fighter Command's initial victory, although not realised at the time, was the postponement of the planned German invasion of Southern England, code-named Sealion, originally set for 15 September.

For Fighter Command, however, the Battle was still very much in progress. Throughout early September, the savage daylight raids on London and other cities continued.

Time and again, the Luftwaffe sent waves of bombers against London, but many were turned back before they could reach their targets, still burning from previous attacks. On one particular day, 8 September, when the Government issued Alert Warning Number 1: 'Invasion imminent and probable within the next 24 hours', the RAF put virtually everything it possessed into the sky, to fight to what everybody expected to be a bitter and bloody end.

However, 15 September was the most critical day, although that did not become apparent until much later. On that day, the

A Spitfire damaged by enemy bombing at Hornchurch on 1 September 1940.

Above. *One aspect of the
Hurricane's operational success
was its comparative ease of
maintenance. Here a Hurricane is
seen being repaired.*

Germans threw their greatest formations of bombers and escorting
fighters against London. In the words of one RAF fighter pilot,
watching them in the air was 'like looking up the Piccadilly Circus
underground escalator'. On that day the entire strength of No. 11
Group of Fighter Command, under Air Vice-Marshal Keith Park
(which bore the brunt of the Battle in the South-East) shattered the
enemy formations and sent them streaming back to France in
disarray. It was during that day, too, that Winston Churchill asked
Park: 'How many fighters have you left?' – meaning how many
reserves – and Park was obliged to answer: 'Sir, there are none'.
Park had been forced to commit all his forces against the enemy,
but he had won the day.

On that day, now traditionally celebrated as Battle of Britain
Day, when the Luftwaffe flung more than 1,000 bombers against
London, Fighter Command shot down 56 German aircraft,
although it was believed at the time that the total was the much
higher one of 185. The British public believed that the Luftwaffe
had been defeated, and there was a great uplift in morale. More
significantly, the Luftwaffe itself began to realise that the tide of
the Battle had turned against it, and that it had failed in its objective
of crushing Fighter Command.

The Battle rumbled on into its final phase in October, with

Fighter Command, weary beyond words, still commanding the skies over Southern England. By the end of that month, the Luftwaffe High Command was obliged to accept that Fighter Command had now also successfully beaten off the daylight attacks on London and other cities, and was clearly victorious overall. Germany was obliged to change its tactics, turning to night attacks on cities by the end of October. Because there had been no time to develop suitable night fighting techniques (which came later in the War), the RAF could initially do little against night bomber raids.

The Battle of Britain had been won. But the toll of casualties was heavy. Later (post-War) German figures gave the Luftwaffe's own losses from 10 July to 31 October 1940, as 1,733 aircraft destroyed and 643 damaged. The RAF, whose actual available fighter strength throughout the Battle varied between 565 aircraft in June to a peak of 758 in August, actually lost between July and October 481 pilots killed, missing or prisoners of war, with another 422 wounded.

Fighter Command had only been able to keep going because of the inflow of young men, many only recently trained, and because Beaverbrook cajoled and even battered the aircraft industry into producing the fighters to replace those lost at such a high rate.

Above. *Pilots of No. 17 Squadron, Flying Officer G. R. Bennett and Flt. Lt. W. J. Harper both wearing Mae Wests, with Sgt. Sherwood (ground staff).*

Above. *The Women's Auxiliary Air Force performed invaluable services during the Second World War in running Communications Centres for all the major Royal Air Force Commands. During the Battle of Britain they worked for long hours daily in the Fighter Command operations control room.*

Opposite. *German bombers in formation en route to Britain in 1940. The picture is an official German one, which was printed the wrong way round!*

Right. *Sector operations centre at RAF Bentley Priory HQ 11 Group. The WAAFs are working on a General Situation Map.*

Above. *A Lockheed Hudson built in the USA seen over the Dunkirk beaches on 31 May 1940. Hudsons were bought for the RAF in quantity just before the Second World War.*

Right. *King George VI signing the Record Book of No. 303 Squadron at Northolt, on 26 September 1940.*

Above. *A familiar scene during the Battle of Britain in 1940 – pilots 'scrambling' to their waiting Hurricanes.*

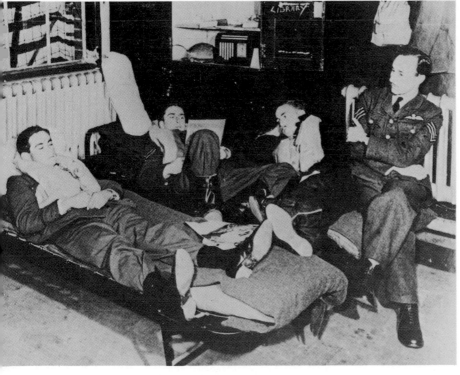

Left. *Pilots of No. 17 Squadron at Martlesham Heath, in the pilots' room awaiting the call to 'scramble', during the early phase of the Battle of Britain, on 20 July 1940.*

King George VI at RAF Northolt on 26 September 1940 talking to AVM Keith Park, AOC 11 Group

During the June–October period, British fighter production (including Beaufighters, Defiants, Hurricanes and Spitfires) totalled 5,185, of which 1,334 were Hurricanes and 731 were Spitfires. Many pilots were shot down, but survived to fly again in a new aircraft, often within hours, and some were shot down several times.

The bald statistics of the Battle cannot therefore disguise the astonishing tales of individual courage, devotion and determination from the young men of Fighter Command, many only between 18 and 21 years of age. The ground crews, too, just as battle weary, worked on deep into the night, every night, to renovate shattered airfields and repair damaged aircraft, ready for the fight next day while the Fighter Controllers and radar personnel also worked round the clock. Without them, Fighter Command could never have survived, Britain would have lost the Battle and probably also the War. It was Winston Churchill who summed it up in his famous phrase, spoken on 20 August before the Battle had reached its peak:

> The gratitude of every home in our island, in our Empire and indeed throughout the world, except in the abodes of the guilty, goes out to the British airmen, who undaunted by the odds, unwearied in their constant challenge and mortal danger, are turning the tide of World War by their prowess and by their devotion. Never in the field of human conflict was so much owed by so many to so few.

Opposite. *The architects of victory in the Battle of Britain: Air Chief Marshal Lord Dowding, Commander-in-Chief, Fighter Command (left), with Air Marshal Sir Trafford Leigh-Mallory, Officer Commanding No. 12 Group, Fighter Command.*

9 The Growth of the RAF and the Strategic Bombing Offensive
1939–1945

FIGHTER COMMAND had won the Battle of Britain, ensuring for this country the chance to carry on the fight against Germany. Now it was the turn of other arms of the RAF to bear their share of the burden, as the War moved into other theatres. Among these, destined to play just as significant a part in the overall struggle, was Bomber Command, whose great strategic offensive against the heartland of Germany was slow to develop but which finally resulted in a massive assault that, in conjunction with the US Eighth Army Air Force, crippled the German economy and made an invaluable contribution to ultimate victory.

Trenchard had initially propounded the philosophy of the offensive, and was largely responsible for the emphasis placed in the RAF on the bomber. From the start, the RAF sought to apply his doctrine. From September 1939 to May 1940, Bomber Command was active, especially in attacks on shipping, but its weapons were not yet geared to the type of assault that was to become necessary. Day bombing at that time was difficult, because of the strength of the fighter and other air defences. The RAF's bombers – Blenheims, Wellingtons, Hampdens and Whitleys – although flown by courageous crews, were not able to inflict on the enemy in the early stages of the War, the massive hammer blows that were necessary to cause serious and lasting damage to the German war effort. Navigational equipment, especially for night operations, was inadequate, the bomb capacity of the aircraft was insufficient, and the aircraft themselves were slow, and very much a prey for German fighters. Losses in the early stages of the War were therefore high, for comparatively small returns.

Nor was there much that Bomber Command could do to help during the Battle of Britain itself, although it kept pounding the invasion ports along the Channel Coast, wrecking many of the barges intended to bring the German armies to Britain's shores. After May 1940, the War Cabinet approved bombing attacks east of the Rhine, which enabled Bomber Command to attack targets in the homeland of Germany itself. There were some benefits. It was not until later that it was realised that the bombing of Berlin by 81 aircraft in August 1940, caused Hitler, in a fury, to divert the Luftwaffe from attacking Fighter Command's airfields and to send his own bombers against London in revenge, thereby giving Fighter Command some respite in the Battle of Britain.

The night bombing offensive of Germany, in addition to doing much to boost British morale when all else was grim and dark, was one of the major factors in the ultimate Allied victory. Day bombing had proved to be extremely costly, because of the effectiveness of the Luftwaffe's fighter squadrons and the anti-aircraft defences. Day bombing was thus not undertaken in any strength until the

This photograph was taken as the attack began on Lorient U-boat bases. The U-boat shelters can be seen on the left, with a block of shelters partly visible through the fins of one of the bombs.

The Armstrong Whitworth
Whitley, although initially used
as a bomber, was also employed
as an anti-submarine warfare
aircraft for Coastal Command. It
also gave valuable service as a
glider-tug and paratroop trainer.

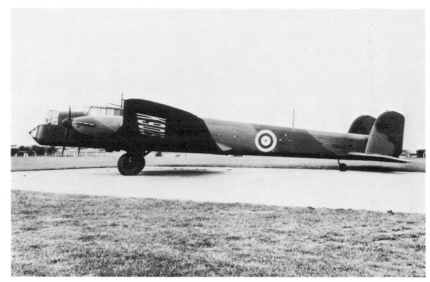

The Handley Page Halifax was
the second of the RAF's four-
engined bombers (arriving soon
after the Short Stirling in late
1940). The Halifax was to
become one of the great bombers of
the war, sharing with the
Lancaster much of the burden of
the strategic bombing offensive,
with over 75,000 sorties, against
the Lancaster's 156,000, between
1941 and 1945.

The de Havilland two-seat twin-
engined Mosquito was one of the
most successful military aircraft
produced for the RAF during the
Second World War. It undertook
a wide variety of missions. The
prototype (bomber version) first
flew on 25 November 1940 at
Hatfield, with the photographic
version flying on 10 June 1941. In
all, 7,781 Mosquitoes were built,
including those built in Canada
and Australia. There was hardly
a task in the RAF which at some
time or another the Mosquito did
not perform, and it was still in
operational service in the early
1950s.

United States entered the War in December 1941 and built up its air bases in Britain. Even then the Fortresses that made up the bulk of its fleet suffered severe casualties until the arrival of the long-range fighters, such as the Merlin-engined Mustang, could provide protective cover deep into Germany and back.

The big change in the tactics of Bomber Command came in late 1941, when after a study of many hundreds of photographs of the damage done by Bomber Command over Germany, it was recognised that hitherto the results were miniscule compared with the heavy expenditure of lives and aircraft. The result was a major effort, authorised by the War Cabinet, to improve Bomber Command. Sir Charles Portal, by then Chief of the Air Staff, wanted a front line force of 4,000 heavy bombers (he never got them: the peak bomber force was to be about 1,700). It was now accepted that the concept of strategic 'area bombing' was a

The Avro Lincoln bomber was developed from the Lancaster, and succeeded it in service. Although it did not see action during the Second World War, it was in service with post-war bomber squadrons through to March 1963.

Right. *Undoubtedly one of the most famous and most successful heavy bombers of all time, the four-engined Avro Lancaster (seen here dropping bombs over the Ruhr) was developed from the earlier unsuccessful twin-engined Manchester. It entered squadron service with No. 44 Squadron at Waddington in late 1941, and after trials, began operations in March 1942.*

Below. *The ubiquitous Vickers Wellington long-range twin-engined night bomber – popularly nicknamed the 'Wimpey' by its crews. In all, 11,461 Wellingtons were built, the last being delivered in October, 1945.*

Bombing up a Lancaster. WAAF Motor Transport driver at the wheel of a tractor which has towed the bomb train from the ammunition dump in August 1944.

primary instrument of warfare – it was really the only way Britain had at that time of carrying on the War effectively.

At the same time, new aircraft types and aids were emerging. The four-engined Stirling entered service in late 1940 and the Handley Page Halifax in early 1941. 'Gee', a new navigational device, came into service in early 1942. But one of the most significant developments was the appointment of Air Marshal Sir Arthur Harris as Air Officer Commanding-in-Chief of Bomber Command, on 23 February 1942. Harris was quickly to prove himself tough and determined, and he has subsequently come to be regarded as one of the greatest commanders of the Second World War, despite post-war criticisms of the bombing policies that he had adopted with the approval of the War Cabinet and the UK's allies, especially the United States of America.

Within three months of Harris taking over, the RAF had delivered its first 1,000 bomber raid, on Cologne, in May 1942, in which nearly 1,500 tons (1,524 tonnes) of bombs were dropped in 90 minutes. It was under Harris that the concept of the 'Path-finder' force emerged (led by Group Captain D. C. T. Bennett), whereby a small force of aircraft sought out and pin-pointed the target with great precision with target-indicator bombs, making the

Opposite. The Germans also hit the UK vigorously with their bombers, especially in the late summer and winter of 1940, when the City of London was severely attacked, with considerable devastation, especially round St. Paul's Cathedral, as this picture shows.

task of the heavy bombers behind that much easier. 'Oboe', another navigation and long-range bombing aid, came into operation late in 1942, whereby range-measurement stations indicated when bombs were to be released.

The biggest single contribution to the success of Bomber Command was the development of the great Lancaster heavy bomber itself. Evolved from the comparatively unsuccessful twin-engined Avro Manchester, the four-engined (Rolls-Royce Merlins) Lancaster first flew in January 1941 and began to move into service from early 1942. Eventually 7,377 were to be built, although many thousands of these were lost in action. From that time on, Bomber Command was on a rising crescendo of power, and many famous exploits were recorded by the Lancaster crews – among them the raid on the Mohne and Eder dams in May 1943, by No. 617 Squadron (The Dam Busters) for which Wing Commander Guy Gibson, the commander, won the Victoria Cross. Lancasters first operated the Pathfinder concept in August 1942, but this duty was later taken over by the Mosquito.

Bomber Command's operations included the attack on Peenemunde on the Baltic, the site of Germany's research for V (for Vengeance) weapons, such as the V-1 flying bombs and the V-2 rockets that were eventually to cause much damage over southern England in late and early 1945.

Lancasters were steadily developed to carry bigger and bigger bombs. Initially capable of a 4,000 lb (1,814 kg) bomb-load, this was

RAF damage at V weapons dump in St Les D'Esseren Caves. This low level air picture shows some of the entrances to the caves blocked by landslides caused by accurate RAF bombing attacks.

progressively increased, to the 8,000 lb (3,629 kg) bombs dropped on Essen in April 1942, to the 12,000 lb (5,443 kg) bombs on the Dortmund-Ems Canal in September 1943 and the deep-penetration 'Tallboy' dropped on the Saumur tunnel in June 1944. Finally, the 'Grand Slam' 22,000-pounder (9,979 kg) was first dropped on the Bielefeld viaduct in March 1945.

The assault by Bomber Command on the German heartland has been described as a series of 'Battles', which indeed it was, although it was really a continuous affair. The Battle of the Ruhr took place from March to July 1943, during which the heavy bombers regularly pounded the industrial heartland of Germany. This was followed by the Battle of Hamburg from July to November 1943, during which that and many other major German cities were progressively devastated, and the Battle of Berlin itself, from November 1943 to March 1944. After the spring of 1944, the battering of Germany continued, especially through the heavy daylight raids of the US Army Air Force, supported by their Merlin-engined long-range Mustang fighters. Bomber Command

Opposite. *After the great Dam Busters' raid on the Mohne and Eder Dams by No. 617 Squadron on 16–17 May 1943, the great wall of the Mohne Dam is seen breached, and the lake behind virtually empty. For his role as the Commander of the Dam Busters, Wing Commander Guy Gibson was awarded the Victoria Cross. The attack severely disrupted the German war production effort in the Ruhr.*

Below. *Mitchell Bomber en route, painted in invasion colours.*

Grandslam bombs weighing 22,000 lbs (9,979 kg) each being prepared for loading into specially adapted Lancasters. Grandslams were used in the Arnsberg viaduct raid on 19 March 1945.

The Lancaster heavy bomber was not only used for attacking land targets, but also for anti-shipping activities, such as the attack on the German battleship Tirpitz in a Norwegian fjord. It was also later used as a maritime reconnaissance aircraft. Here a Lancaster is seen being loaded with mines.

Lancaster S For Sugar, now in the RAF Museum at Hendon, is famous for being the Lancaster with the most operational sorties to its credit – 137 missions with Bomber Command.

Airmen servicing a Halifax bomber whilst farmworkers bring in the harvest. The Handley Page Halifax, which shared the burden of the RAF's strategic bombing offensive over Germany, flew more than 75,000 sorties from the time it entered service in late 1940 through to the end of the war in 1945. It also served with Coastal Command and the Airborne Forces. In all, 6,176 Halifaxes were built for the RAF, and it continued to serve well into the post-war period, particularly in Coastal Command, and as a transport aircraft as well as with the Airborne Forces for paratroop and glider-towing duties.

itself was required to pound targets associated with the forth-coming 'Overlord' invasion of France in June of that year.

After the reconquest of France, Bomber Command returned to the assault on Germany, its first priorities being the destruction of the German petroleum industry, rail and waterborne transport systems, armaments production factories and other installations vital to the German war effort. By this time, the pounding of Germany was going on round the clock, with the US Army Air Force hitting targets by day, and Bomber Command slamming them by night. With improved navigation aids, and the virtual destruction of the German fighter defences, Bomber Command and the Eighth USAAF were able to make precise bombing attacks by both night and day on specifically selected targets, calculated to do the maximum damage to the German war effort.

It was during 1944, in July, that the RAF attained its peak strength of the Second World War, with 1,185,833 personnel, of whom 1,011,427 were men and 174,406 women. In October 1944, the heaviest bomber raid of the War was made, during which 1,576 aircraft dropped 5,453 tons (5,540 tonnes) on German territory, with 4,547 tons (4,620 tonnes) being dropped on the industrial city of Duisburg in a single night.

The build up of the bomber offensive can be gauged from the fact that in the first three years of the War, only 121,298 tons (123,244 tonnes) of bombs were dropped on Germany. In 1943, Bomber Command dropped nearly 157,500 tons (160,026 tonnes), and in 1944, more than 525,000 tons (533,421 tonnes). Altogether, in 392,137 Bomber Command sorties, just under one million tons of bombs were dropped. Of these sorties, Lancasters made over 156,000, the rest being mostly by Stirlings and Halifaxes.

The casualties, inevitably, were enormous. During the entire Second World War, the RAF lost 70,253 personnel killed in action, and 22,294 wounded. Of those killed, no less than 47,000, or 67 per cent, were air-crew from Bomber Command, with another 18,000 wounded, taken prisoner or missing, of whom about 13,000 were prisoners of war. It can be argued that these RAF personnel paid the personal sacrifices for the eventually low level of casualties incurred during the Normandy invasion.

Subsequently, the Bomber Command offensive has been the subject of much debate, during which it has been alleged that it was less effective than was believed at the time. The truth is that it made a massive contribution to the destruction of the German war effort, especially in the later stages of the War, without which it is likely that hostilities would have continued for much longer than they did. It also contributed greatly to the destruction of German civilian morale, while it gave a massive boost to the morale of the British population, who felt the Allies were really hitting the enemy where it hurt him most.

Marshal of the RAF Sir Arthur Harris has himself summed up the role of Bomber Command by pointing to the comments of leading German figures. Albert Speer, Hitler's Armaments Minister, for example, made the point that the strategic offensive by Bomber Command was 'the greatest lost battle for Germany of the whole war'. Again, the German Field Marshal, Rommel, told the German High Command: 'Stop the bombing or we cannot win. All we can get by going on is to lose another city every night'. The German General who surrendered Boulogne with 8,000 troops, said: 'One is driven to despair when at the mercy of the RAF without defence'.

It has also been subsequently alleged that the offensive was inhumane, in that inevitably large numbers of German civilians, estimated at over half a million, died. But the fact that cannot be escaped is that Britain and the Commonwealth, along with their Allies, were fighting a War begun by a ruthless enemy, which had quickly overrun and enslaved most of Europe, perpetrating many cruelties and killing millions. There was no other way in which Britain could prosecute the War effectively, after 1940, other than by bombing Germany.

The criticisms of the Bomber offensive have always been made with hindsight by people who, without the wartime achievements of Bomber Command, would not today be enjoying the freedom to make their criticisms. Many thousands of brave young men died in Bomber Command in the firm and just belief that they were fighting to end a vicious and evil scourge that had already paralysed much of the Western World, and threatened to enslave Britain as well. They did not die in vain.

The Battle of the Atlantic and Coastal Command

1939–1945

10

WHILE THE STORIES of the Battle of Britain and Bomber Command have been told frequently and at great length, that of Coastal Command has had less exposure. It is nonetheless a vital one in the history of the RAF. Without the achievements of Coastal Command, the great, unrelenting Battle of the Atlantic – which began as soon as War broke out and only ended when the Germans surrendered – would never have been won, and the Allies would assuredly have lost the War.

The escalation of the War at sea was rapid world-wide. In 1939, on the day War was declared, the liner, *Athenia*, was sunk. For the next four months, the total of Allied and neutral merchant shipping lost was 755,000 tons (767,110 tonnes). In 1940, this rose to nearly 4m. tons (4.06m. tonnes), and in 1941 further to over 4.3m. tons (4.37m. tonnes). In 1942, it reached the staggering figure of nearly 7.8m. tons (7.92m. tonnes), when the Battle of the Atlantic was at its height, and thereafter, as the Allies began to gain the ascendancy, it fell away sharply in 1943 to about 3.2m. tons (3.25m. tonnes), and to a third of that in 1944. By 1945, with the Allies in total command of the Western seaboard of Europe, and only a few U-boats left at sea, the shipping losses fell sharply to 439,000 tons (446,041 tonnes). But the figures show clearly that the Battle at sea was an unceasing, unrelenting struggle, against appalling odds, and with all the forces of nature as well as man flung against the Allies.

The shipping losses inevitably escalated as the Germans occupied the Channel ports in 1940, thereby gaining massive U-boat harbours and building yards. At the same time, however, as the Allies put an increasing effort into the struggle, the U-boat losses themselves rose sharply. U-boats sunk in the Atlantic by various means – ships, aircraft, mines, and Allied submarines – rose from 9 in 1939 to 22 in 1940; 35 in 1941; 85 in 1942; 237 in 1943; 240 in 1944, and 153 in 1945, a total of 781. Together with

Opposite above. One of the first German airfields used for jet fighters: the runway at Rheine, West of Osnabruck, showing the scorch-marks where Messerschmidt 262s, the first German jet fighters, had taken off.

Opposite below. The Vickers Valiant was the first of the famous 'triad' of jet V-bombers to enter service with the RAF, joining No. 138 Squadron at Gaydon, Warwickshire, in January 1955.

The Short Sunderland is one of the most famous of all the RAF's aircraft. Entering service in 1938, this aircraft was still operational in the mid 1950s. Throughout the war the Sunderland was one of the mainstays of Coastal Command's bitter and unceasing struggle against enemy submarines, while after the war it performed well in support of United Nations forces in the Korean War, as well as in the Berlin Airlift, and against terrorists in Malaya. By the time production ended in 1946, 739 Sunderlands had been built.

U-boats sunk elsewhere, in all 866 enemy submarines (excluding Japanese) were destroyed throughout the War, of which 243 were credited to the RAF. In addition, 1,518 surface vessels were sunk by the RAF, amounting to over 1.75m. tons (1.78m. tonnes).

Coastal Command aircraft were able to track U-boats by radar with the introduction of 'ASV' radar – Air to Surface Vessel – and attack accordingly. Also, in 1942, the 'Leigh Light', invented by Squadron Leader Leigh of Coastal Command, enabled attacking aircraft to track U-boats with ASV, and then suddenly switch on an intense light beam to illumine their attacks. It became the standard equipment in Wellingtons, Catalinas and Liberators of Coastal Command. The equipment was used extensively to attack U-boats in the Bay of Biscay, where they tended to surface at night.

Another factor behind the late ascendancy over the submarines was that up to 1942, the types of aircraft available to the Allies did not have sufficient range to provide air cover for the convoys all the way across the Atlantic. It was not until the very long range versions of the Liberators, Halifaxes and Sunderland aircraft became available that convoys were able to sail in comparative safety all the way across the Atlantic. The Coastal Command aircraft supplemented the Allied navies in the protection of convoys.

Coastal Command's problems were not just to find U-boats and attack them: they also had to contend with marauding enemy aircraft sent to attack *them*. There were many reports of Coastal Command aircraft being attacked, but in general, the air-crews were more than able to fend these off, and with the support of land-based Beaufighters from the UK, the marauders came to be regarded as more of a nuisance than a major menace.

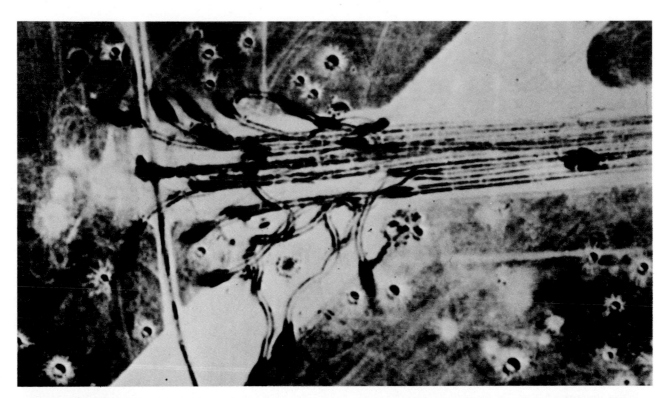

Right. *Loading up a Typhoon rocket-firing fighter. The Hawker Typhoon was a formidable weapon in the Second Tactical Air Force's fighter-bomber wings in the Allied advance through France and the Low Countries in 1944.*

Below. *The German battleship* Gneisenau *under attack in Brest Harbour by Halifaxes of Bomber Command in a daylight raid in December 1941.*

Left. *The de Havilland single-engined Venom, although designed during the war, did not enter service until 1946, but it performed valuable service both at home and overseas (especially in the Far East and Germany) in a wide variety of roles, until the late 1950s.*

Below. *The Avro Shackleton four piston-engined long-range maritime reconnaissance aircraft has been one of the longest-serving aircraft in the RAF, entering service in 1951. It is still operating today in the Airborne Early Warning (AEW) role, although now being replaced by AEW Nimrods.*

A more serious problem was the anti-aircraft fire thrown against the attacking Allied aircraft by the submarines caught on the surface, and many attacking aircraft were destroyed, after having pressed home their own attacks with considerable courage. Eventually, in the early part of 1944, the U-boats resorted to the 'schnorkel' technique of taking in air whilst still submerged, and this led to a temporary setback for the RAF in its war against the submarine, although not all of the U-boats were equipped in this way.

One of the most famous actions of the Battle of the Atlantic in which Coastal Command played a part was the sinking of the German battleship, *Bismarck* in 1941. Having herself sunk the British battle cruiser, *Hood*, in the Denmark Strait and driven on into the Atlantic, the *Bismarck* eluded the battleships of the Royal Navy until a Coastal Command Catalina on 26 May, flying from Loch Erne in Northern Ireland, spotted the quarry 690 miles west of Brest, heading for the French coast. Fleet Air Arm Swordfish aircraft from the carrier *Ark Royal* opened the attack, damaging the enemy's steering gear, but finally the Navy's heavy guns and torpedoes destroyed the *Bismarck* which rolled over and sank with

Opposite above. The first jet fighter to enter service with the RAF (in 1944) was the twin-engined Gloster Meteor (left), followed by the de Havilland single-engined Vampire in 1946 (top).

Opposite below. US-built Phantom fighters with Rolls-Royce Spey jet engines joined the RAF in the late 1960s and are still in service with the RAF in the Air Defence role. The two pictures show the marked development of combat aircraft over a period of twenty years.

Coastal Command's first kill of 1944. The Sunderlands' gunners put a final burst of fire across the approaching U-boats. Survivors can be seen in the water (bottom right). A few seconds later the U-Boat disappeared beneath the surface, exactly six and a half minutes after the first sighting.

heavy loss of life among her crew. The loss of the *Bismarck* helped considerably to change the Allies' prospects in the Battle of the Atlantic, virtually removing the threat of surface warships, leaving it to the enemy's U-boats to carry on the attack.

A significant development in the war against the submarine was that from October 1942, Coastal Command was able to use the Portuguese Azores, thereby helping to close the southern gap in air cover for convoys. Slowly, the net was being pulled round the U-boats.

The enemy, however, was resilient and resourceful, and persistently sought to intensify his activities, not only in the Atlantic, but along the coasts of Europe. But by now Coastal Command crews were becoming highly skilled in detecting and attacking U-boats, and the sinking rate continued to rise. When Air Marshal Slessor took over Coastal Command in March 1943, many of the developments carefully prepared earlier were coming to fruition. These included additional medium-range squadrons, releasing longer-range aircraft for attacks in mid-Atlantic, while new types of rockets, depth charges, radar and searchlights all helped to improve the efficiency of the anti-submarine battle. The climax of the Battle of the Atlantic really occurred in May 1943, when Allied shipping losses fell off, and U-boat sinkings increased. The Battle, however, was very much an inter-service affair, probably one of the finest examples throughout the War of co-operation between the Royal Navy and the RAF, united in a common fray.

By the time of the Allied landings in Normandy in June 1944, the war on the U-boats had reached the point where they were virtually unable to prevent the vast Allied armadas from crossing the Channel. The U-boats were also ineffective against the subsequent supply lines from Britain to France, through which flowed all the sinews of war to keep the invasion forces at the peak of their efficiency. Bomber Command's continued poundings of the submarine harbours and building yards along the coast of Europe supported the joint efforts of Coastal Command and the Royal Navy, so that even when in harbour no U-boat was safe.

Moreover, the Allied armies broke out of their D-Day beachheads in Normandy, and captured one by one the great French U-boat ports in Brittany, at Cherbourg and Le Havre. So the home bases for enemy submarines were progressively reduced, while the German shipyards were also battered.

The activities of the U-boats continued through to the very end of the War – the last being sunk by a Catalina of No. 210 Squadron on 7 May 1945 – and no-one in Coastal Command would ever deny that throughout the War it had been obliged to fight a very tough, resourceful and ruthless enemy.

The RAF Overseas

1939–1945

11

During the Second World War, the RAF played a prominent role in the war overseas, which eventually became virtually global. RAF units fought not only on the Continent of Europe, in the Mediterranean and the Middle East, but also in parts of Africa, India and South-East Asia, although in the Pacific much of the air war was conducted by the US armed forces operating from aircraft carriers and island bases.

The RAF's major contribution to the War in overseas theatres was in the Mediterranean, primarily along the North African littoral to start with, but later extending to Sicily and the Italian peninsula itself. The RAF, at the outbreak of war, was firmly established in Egypt, Palestine, Transjordan, Iraq, Aden, East Africa, the Sudan and Malta. This was a result of the continuation through the 1930s of Trenchard's original policy of using the RAF as the principal policing agent in those territories where terrain was difficult for normal overland operations. In those vast areas, the RAF collectively by June 1940 had about 29 squadrons, with some 300 first-line aircraft.

After the Italian entry into the War in mid-1940, the whole of the North African littoral, except for Egypt, became hostile territory, and the Mediterranean itself became highly dangerous for shipping – indeed, much U-boat activity was centred in the Mediterranean, and initially Allied shipping losses there were heavy. As a result, the main supply line for aircraft destined for the Middle East became the long way round, via Takoradi on the west coast of Africa. Aircraft were shipped to that port, where they were re-assembled, and flown across Africa via Accra, Lagos, Kano, Maiduguri, Fort Lamy, El Gemeina, El Fasher, El Obeid, Khartoum, Wadi Halfa, into Egypt to Cairo. Eventually, from June 1941, aircraft were also delivered to the Middle East direct from the USA via the South Atlantic ferry route.

The role of the RAF in the Mediterranean campaigns was

*A heavy attack on a Japanese
Airfield near Rangoon. Two RAF
Liberators over the target drop
bombs through the clouds on to the
airfield below.*

*A Princess Mary's Royal Air
Force Nursing Service Nursing
Officer in a Far East field
hospital.*

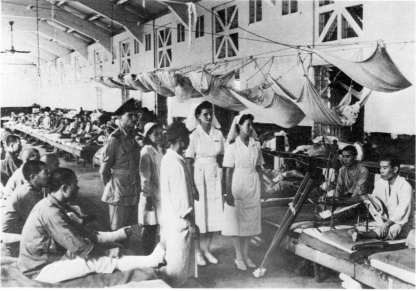

critical to the entire success of the British, and eventually the Allied, campaigns in North Africa. Without the ultimate command of the air that the RAF eventually won in the Mediterranean theatre, it is doubtful if the armies on the ground would have achieved the successes they did.

When the Italians entered the War, there was a series of major battles. In the North African littoral, the British forces pushed the Italians back to Benghazi, while they also cleared them from Abyssinia and East Africa. In these battles the RAF played a major role. But the Germans came to the aid of the Italians, first in North Africa in January 1941, and then they invaded Greece, forcing the limited British forces there back across the Mediterranean to Egypt, with heavy losses. General Irwin Rommel, the 'Desert Fox', with large numbers of fresh troops, swept across North Africa, driving the British forces back to Egypt. In the spring and summer of 1941, there were other difficulties to deal with. The rebellion of Rashid Ali in Iraq resulted in a siege of the RAF base at Habbaniya, but with limited reinforcements of Wellingtons from Shaibah and some Naval Swordfish aircraft from the carrier, *Hermes*, the rebellion was put down. The North African campaigns were very fluid, with each side successively driving the other back, until eventually, the British, forced back into Egypt, stood firm along a line from El Alamein to the Quattara depression.

In all these land battles, the RAF fought with great heroism, in considerable difficulties caused by dust, the changing nature of the war on the ground, and supply problems. The squadrons included not only British airmen, but also South African, Free French, Australians, Greeks and Yugoslavs. Almost anyone who could fly and wanted to fight found a home and a welcome in the Desert Air Force, and there was an enormous camaraderie amongst the squadrons. In the same way that the ground forces, eventually under Montgomery in the Eighth Army, came to regard themselves as the élite of the Army, so did the pilots of the Desert Air Force come to regard themselves as an élite of the air. After all, they had been fighting the enemy directly and continuously since the Italians entered the War.

At this time, Malta, the vital strategic island lying astride the Allies' Mediterranean sea routes from west to east, and the Axis powers' supply lines from north to south, came under fierce attack from the Germans. In the Battle of Malta, the RAF, heavily outnumbered, played a major role. At one time, the only aircraft left available were three battered Gladiators, nicknamed Faith, Hope and Charity – although eventually reinforcements of Hurricanes and other aircraft were to arrive. It was essential that the island be held by the British at all costs, but the price was heavy, with over 11,000 tons (11,176 tonnes) of bombs raining down on the island

Mr. Churchill acknowledging greetings as he walks away from the aircraft in which he flew from England to the Middle East.

in the first few months of 1942. The gallantry of the population in withstanding this sustained assault, led to the island being awarded the George Cross, by King George VI.

The major change in the fortunes of the British forces in the Western Desert came with the Second Battle of Alamein in October–November 1942, with General Sir Bernard Montgomery commanding the Eighth Army, and Air Marshal Sir Arthur Coningham in command of the Desert Air Force. At this time, the RAF had about 100 front-line squadrons in the Desert Air Force, with about 1,200 aircraft. Working together, these commanders perfected the collaboration between land and air forces, laying the foundations for later co-operation in the assault on Europe. The forces of Rommel were shattered, with the RAF dominating the skies over the battlefield. The Battle, one of the most famous of the Second World War, led to Rommel's retreat across the Western Desert until he was finally squeezed between the Eighth Army at his heels and the approaching Allied forces which had invaded Morocco and Algeria in 'Operation Torch'.

One outcome of 'Torch' was that the entire Allied air forces in the Mediterranean were placed under Air Chief Marshal Sir Arthur Tedder in a new Mediterranean Air Command. At that time, the Allies had a first-line strength of more than 3,200 aircraft, against about 500 for the Luftwaffe and about 450 from the Italian

Regia Aeronautica. The end of the war in Africa came when the German forces had been trapped by the Allied Armies and could no longer be supplied by air from Europe. The German commander, von Arnim, could neither advance nor retreat, or even evacuate. There was nowhere to go, and he surrendered. By May 1943, the Allied forces commanded the entire North African shore from Casablanca to the Eastern Mediterranean.

Thereafter followed the invasion of Sicily, from 10 July 1943, to 17 August, during which time the air battle was fought by the combined RAF and US Army Tactical Air Forces, under Sir Arthur Tedder. By winning air superiority over the battlefield, the air forces were able to provide the ground forces with security from enemy air attack. But the losses were heavy – the Allies lost 400 aircraft, although they destroyed or captured 1,850 enemy aircraft.

There followed the long and painful slogging match with the enemy up the Italian peninsula during the appalling winter of 1943–44, during which an immense effort was made by the Allied air forces – a factor often forgotten in studies of the Italian campaigns. The Allies had over 3,000 first-line aircraft at their disposal, and the Luftwaffe was unable to intervene effectively owing to the Allies' air superiority. Air power was critical to the success of the entire Italian campaign. Moreover, with the capture of the Foggia airfields in September 1943, the Allies were able to launch heavy

A flying boat base in Ceylon. WAAF equipment assistants preparing spare parts for a flying boat moored on the lagoon in May 1945.

bomber attacks from the Italian peninsula into Central Europe, thereby making an invaluable contribution to the combined bomber offensive. After the fall of Rome on 4 June 1944, there was no longer any Luftwaffe opposition, and the tactical air forces were able to concentrate entirely on providing ground support for the land battles. As the Battle for Italy moved into its final phase in late 1944, the Allies had over 10,000 aircraft in the Mediterranean Allied Air Forces (MAAF), of which 5,400 were operational, including some 2,000 from the RAF.

This weight of air power in Italy was also helpful to the partisan campaign in Yugoslavia, across the Adriatic. Operating from Italian bases, the Balkan air force, built up in 1943–44, was of major assistance in the struggle to liberate Yugoslavia.

The other great arena for the RAF overseas was in South-East Asia. The entry of Japan into the War on 7 December 1941, brought with it many air attacks throughout South-East Asia and the Pacific, including those on Malaya, Singapore and Hong Kong. By the following February, the Japanese had captured all of Malaya and Singapore, and had swept through virtually the whole of South-East Asia and the Western Pacific, bringing them to the

The capture of Derna, near Tripoli. Pilots and ground crew examine the wreckage of an enemy aircraft at Derna.

borders of India. There was virtually no British air opposition – there were very few aircraft that could be spared from Europe and the Middle East.

There followed one of the most difficult, painful and long-drawn-out wars of attrition against an enemy strongly dug into jungle defences and with massive air power at his command. The Allies, working under the most appalling conditions of tropical weather and almost impossible terrain, managed to keep the Japanese from invading India. With the Allies fighting grim battles in the Middle East and the North Atlantic, and building up the strength of Bomber Command for the ultimately paralysing attacks on Germany, the war in South-East Asia seemed very far away, and initially few resources could be spared for it. The build-up of RAF strength in India and Ceylon (the closest bases to the Japanese) was slow – from 26 operational squadrons in June 1942, it had climbed only to 38 a year later, and then to 64 by the spring of 1944. Yet the RAF had many important parts to play in the Far East. It was largely the RAF's duty to co-operate with the Army in the defence of India and to provide maritime air support for the Royal Navy in order to win back control of the Indian Ocean. The RAF co-operated with the Army in offensive operations – first in Arakan and then in Burma, where air supply was essential, first for the Chindits and then for Sir William Slim's 14th Army. It also prepared for the eventual invasion of Malaya, scheduled for September 1945, and for the Tiger Force, which was to join the US Army Air Force in bombing Japan.

Slowly, as the Allied air strength improved, mastery in the air was won over Burma, enabling the ground forces to force the Japanese back through the jungle. Rangoon fell to the British in May 1945.

It was left to the US air forces on aircraft carriers and island bases to fight the great Battles of the Western Pacific, which did so much to destroy the Japanese command of the air. These battles are not part of the history of the RAF, but nonetheless they helped considerably to drain Japanese air power away from the land-based battles in South-East Asia, and to that extent they helped the RAF considerably.

Another great achievement of the South-East Asian campaign, of which little is said, is that during it a much closer liaison was developed between the air forces and the troops on the ground. The ground forces depended almost entirely upon the air for their supplies and communications, and for evacuating the wounded. It was a tightly organised, cohesive collaboration that worked well, and much of the foundation for subsequent techniques of Army and air collaboration on the battlefield was laid at that time.

12 *The Final Assault*

1944–1945

IN THE PREPARATIONS for the invasion of the Continent on 6 June 1944, all the resources of the UK-based air forces were switched to the attack on France. There was a combined assault designed to remove the Luftwaffe from the skies – which it did – and to isolate the invasion area.

For a considerable time prior to that, however, while Bomber Command was pounding Germany, the formidable weight of the Tactical Air Forces in the UK, primarily Fighter Command but aided by the US Army Air Force, had been directed to harassing the enemy on the near-Continent. Fighter Command's massive 'sweeps' over France and the Low Countries became famous, attacking 'anything that moves'. From the spring of 1944, however, the weight of Bomber Command was also turned on France, against rail communications, coastal radar stations, and on any targets that conceivably could be used by the Germans to reinforce their own armies in France. This did not mean that the attack on Germany itself was ended: rather that, for a brief period, it was reduced in scale, although it remained massive.

When D-Day occurred on 6 June, the invasion of France was supported by over 14,000 first-line aircraft in the Allied air forces, resulting in absolute air supremacy over the battlefield. On D-Day itself, the RAF flew 5,656 sorties. It was soon after D-Day that the RAF actually reached its peak Second World War strength of 1,185,833 personnel, of whom 1,011,427 were men and 174,406 were women.

By September, it was decided that the resources of Bomber Command and the US Eighth Army Air Force could be put to better use in support of the overall war effort, and control of Bomber Command was restored by the Supreme Allied Commander, General Eisenhower, to the Combined Chiefs of Staff. As a result, Bomber Command was given a new directive, to attack oil installations, the subsidiary targets being rail and water transport,

military installations such as airfields, and also major production targets. Bomber Command's abilities were now fine-tuned: in addition to the area bombing capability with the massive force of Lancasters, Stirlings, Halifaxes and Mosquitoes, it had perfected its techniques of precision bombing so that it could destroy targets hitherto considered impracticable. Bomber Command's contribution to victory in this period until the end of the War has rightly been described as 'decisive'.

The RAF transport force also played a major role in the advance of the Allied Armies through the Continent en route to Germany. The RAF had developed considerable skills in dropping parachute troops and towing gliders for airborne attacks. These were used extensively in the assault on Arnhem and Nijmegen in 'Operation Market Garden' in September 1944.

The RAF also played a vital role in another area: the destruction of the V-1 'Flying Bombs' that began to rain on south-eastern England in the summer of 1944. RAF fighter pilots discovered that they could fly both their Spitfires and their newly-acquired Meteor jet fighters alongside these unmanned weapons, and tip them over by touching them underneath their wings, to crash harmlessly before they could reach London. Many others of the 1,400 of these weapons launched against Britain were shot down by fighters, or by anti-aircraft fire from the ground, and many fell into the English Channel. Thus, the RAF's role in defeating the Flying Bomb menace was significant. What really ended that menace, however, was the major break-out by the Allies from the Normandy beachheads, and their subsequent race along the Channel coast, capturing the Flying Bomb sites and destroying them. A more formidable 'Vengeance' weapon, the V-2 rockets were launched from Holland and the fighters could do nothing about them. It was left to Bomber Command to pound the launch sites, supply lines and manufacturing plants, thereby severely restricting the flow of

Airspeed Horsa Gliders waiting for the Airborne assault on Hitler's 'Fortress Europa' to begin.

Stirling and Halifax Glider Tugs towing Horsa gliders. Conceived well before the Second World War, the Short Stirling four-engined bomber entered service with No. 7 Squadron at Leeming in August 1940. Although not built in anything like the same numbers as the Lancaster and Halifax – over 2,360 were built in all – the Stirling, in its various versions, nevertheless performed well as a bomber. Towards the end of the War it was primarily employed as a glider tug and a transport aircraft.

missiles. Nevertheless, the V-2 rockets remained a menace to lives and property until well into 1945, when those sites also fell into Allied hands.

It was in the late summer of 1944 that one of the most significant developments in the history of the RAF, and indeed of air power generally, occurred, with the introduction into squadron service of the first jet fighter, the Gloster Meteor, initially with the Rolls-Royce Welland engine. Developed under conditions of considerable secrecy during the early years of the War, the first British aircraft using jet propulsion, the Gloster E28/39 using the Whittle W-1 engine, successfully made its maiden flight on the evening of 15 May 1941, from RAF Cranwell, with P. E. G. Sayer, Gloster's chief test pilot, at the controls.

The jet engine itself was the work of Frank Whittle (later Air Commodore Sir Frank). He had begun work on the idea of jet propulsion as far back as the early 1920s, when he was a cadet at the RAF College, Cranwell, later publishing his fundamental thesis on the gas-turbine as a power-plant for aircraft in 1928.

The story of Whittle's long and painful struggle, against official disinterest, to develop an effective jet engine for aircraft propulsion, has been told admirably by himself and by others who worked with him. For our purposes it is enough to know that before the Second World War official interest in it had at last strenghtened and Whittle was able to work with greater encouragement, although still with insufficient resources. He ran his first jet engine on the test bed on 12 April 1937, and the long period of subsequent development resulted in the Gloster E28/39 and the W-1 in 1941. Thereafter, work on further developing the engine and an aircraft to use it continued at an accelerating pace, resulting in the introduction of the Welland-powered Meteors into squadron service in July 1944 – in time for the squadrons to use them against the Flying Bombs.

The arrival of the Meteors was only just in time, however, for the Germans had also been working on jet propulsion, and the Messerschmidt Me-262 came into operational service at about the same time as the Meteor, with a slightly better performance. This led to the rapid improvement of the Meteor's own performance, with the development of the Rolls-Royce Derwent engine – one of the most successful jet engines of all time, with over 9,700 being built in Britain (and eventually also Belgium) before production ended in 1954.

The jet engine is really the major link between the RAF at the end of the War and the early period of the peace. For, as the War drew to its inevitable close in Western Europe, with the eventual crushing of the German air force, and the establishment of absolute mastery over the skies of Western Europe, many in the RAF were

already thinking of what was to come, including, for example, the need to concentrate more forces in the final effort to crush Japan.

By V-E day, the RAF possessed a total strength of 55,469 aircraft, of which 9,200 were first-line (bombers and fighters). It had grown to a total strength of nearly 1.2m. men and women, and it was the second largest air force in the world, after that of the US. The Soviet Air Force, although very large, especially in fighters, did not reach the same size as either the RAF or the US air forces. The RAF's casualties had been massive, however, with over 70,000

A few hours after RAF Bomber Command's attack on industrially important Stuttgart on the night of 20/21 February 1944. Smoke pours from many buildings in the plants of Robert Bosch (magnetos and ignition equipment – top right), Leichmetallbau GmbH (sheetmetal) and Wurtembirgishe Elekrizitats (electrical equipment – bottom left).

RAF and Dominion pilots on an airstrip in France after the D-Day invasion.

killed in action, including 47,000 in Bomber Command. But the service stood poised on the verge of a new era, with the exciting possibilities of the jet age before it.

Throughout the war, the RAF had undertaken many other tasks, all of which were vital to the overall victory. These included minelaying, especially in inshore waters off the coast of occupied Europe, undertaken throughout the War with considerable success in the destruction of enemy shipping. Photographic reconnaissance was another skill in which the Spitfire and Mosquito played major roles, and which was essential for all the other tasks. Special operations, such as landing or collection of agents in enemy territory were also vital. The ferrying of new aircraft across the Atlantic to the UK, and from the UK to other destinations, were tasks often carried out by women with immense courage and devotion to duty.

Behind all these activities lay the hundreds of thousands of unsung heroes of the war-time RAF – the men and women who serviced the aircraft, manned the radars, fed, administered and trained the men. In any fighting force, far more people are involved in the mundane jobs behind the front line than are involved in the fighting, and although in some cases (although by no means all) their tasks in the Second World War were safer than those of the aircrew, they were nonetheless vital, and without them, the aircrew could never have performed their own feats of heroism.

Into the Jet Age

1945–1970

13

THE FIRST TASK of the RAF in the peace after 1945, was to repatriate many thousands of prisoners of war, and to help undertake the Allied occupation of Germany. But the inevitable rundown of the force began, with many thousands of airmen being returned to civilian life, and many squadrons being disbanded. Nonetheless, it was not all a story of dismantling the superb machine that had been so painstakingly created over nearly six years of War.

There were still some major tasks to be undertaken. Although it was peace-time, it was an uneasy period, with a massive and sullen Soviet Union standing across half of Europe, confronting the Allies. The remarkable political changes that occurred in Europe in the period immediately after the War, with the increasing awareness of the hostility of the Soviet Union towards the West, made it clear that the Allies would need to retain forces of considerable size to protect themselves against any attack. As a result, the RAF remained a tough, vigorous force, albeit much smaller than during the War.

A manifestation of the uneasiness of peace came in 1948. On 24 June, as a result of Soviet action in Berlin, virtually cutting that city off from the West, the Allies resorted to a massive airlift. By the time this operation, 'Plainfare', ended in May 1949, the RAF, using up to 40 Yorks, 50 Dakotas, 14 Hastings and 10 Sunderland flying boats, had flown over 18.2m. miles (29.29m. km) in nearly 66,000 flights, airlifting 400,000 tons (406,416 tonnes) of stores and over 67,000 passengers. Even after the Soviet Blockade was lifted on 12 May 1949, the RAF continued its share of the airlift so as to build up stocks of food and other supplies in Berlin.

It was at this time that the Allies decided to set up the North Atlantic Treaty Organisation (1949) for their mutual protection against the might of the Soviet Union. At the same time, UK Government decisions to embark upon nuclear weapons, and a force of V-bombers with which to carry them, were also taken.

Opposite. *The unique vertical take-off and landing British Aerospace Harrier close-support fighter can operate from small clearings or other spaces, close to the battle front.*

From the time the first atomic bombs were dropped by the Allies in 1945 on the Japanese cities of Hiroshima and Nagasaki, it was clear the world had entered the new era of nuclear warfare, and this fact has played an all-important role in military thinking ever since. Britain, in the immediate post-war period, developed its own atomic weapons, and an RAF team assembled the first British A-bomb tested in the Monte Bello islands of the Pacific in October 1952. The first British atomic bomb dropped from an aircraft was in tests made with a Valiant of No. 49 Squadron at Maralinga, South Australia, in October 1956. The Valiant was the first of a new generation of bombers – the famous triad of 'V-bombers' – to enter service, with No. 138 Squadron at Gaydon in 1955.

Progressively it became apparent that atomic bombs were not likely to be sufficient to maintain Britain's position in the front rank of nuclear nations in the post-war world, and so the more powerful H-bomb was developed, the first being dropped (also from a Valiant of No. 49 Squadron) at Christmas Island in the Pacific in May 1957.

From this point on, the RAF became responsible for carrying the 'Strategic Nuclear Deterrent' – the H-bombs that comprised Britain's ability, if attacked, to retaliate massively with nuclear weapons, making a major contribution to the overall retaliatory capabilities of the North Atlantic Treaty Organisation. The RAF's deterrent was carried in the form of the Blue Steel nuclear stand-off bomb, borne by some (but not all) of the V-bomber force.

Below. *The Blackburn Beverley was the largest aircraft of its type to be built in Britain. It was specially designed for dropping Army equipment through rear loading doors. It had a payload of 22 tons, and a freight load of nearly 6,000 cu ft.*

The Avro Vulcan Delta-winged bomber entered service with No. 230 Operational Conversion Unit at Waddington in May 1956, followed by the Handley Page Victor crescent-winged bomber (No. 232 OCU at Gaydon) in November 1957. The V-bomber force grew progressively stronger and increasingly

Opposite above. *The British Aerospace Jet Provost Mark 5 basic trainer seen over the Fylingdales Ballistic Missile Early Warning Station in Yorkshire.*

Below. *Harrier GR.Mark 3s from No. 1 Squadron, Wittering.*

Left. *The Westland Sea King helicopter performs inavaluable service in the RAF's Search and Rescue units round Britain's coasts, frequently operating in some of the most appalling weather conditions.*

Below. *British Aerospace Hawks of the RAF's Red Arrows aerobatic formation team, seen in line abreast during a recent tour of the Middle East.*

The British Aerospace Hawk is used for a wide variety of training roles, including tactical weapons training. This aircraft is also now to be used for training pilots of the US Navy.

Right. *The British Aerospace Bulldog is the RAF's initial basic trainer. It is also used by fifteen other air forces round the world.*

The Avro Shackleton four-engined
anti-submarine reconnaissance
aircraft was developed from the
Lincoln bomber. It first flew on
9 March 1949.

The Gloster E28/39 was an
experimental aircraft, best known
as the airframe used to test the
Whittle W-1, the original jet
engine.

The English Electric Canberra
was the first light jet bomber to be
built in Britain. The prototype
flew at Warton, Lancashire, on
13 May 1949, and the type
entered RAF service as a bomber
with No. 101 Squadron at
Binbrook in May 1951. It was
subsequently also employed as a
photo-reconnaissance aircraft.
Having been successively
improved in terms of both high-
altitude performance and range/
payload, the Canberra became
one of the most ubiquitous of all
RAF aircraft.

Right. *One of the least successful of the RAF's post-war jet fighters, the Vickers Supermarine Swift, had only a limited production run in its various versions, and did not remain long in service. It was the first swept-wing fighter to enter service, in February 1954, but only one squadron used the aircraft as an interceptor, and it was withdrawn from Fighter Command in 1955. It was later used in the FR-5 version as a tactical reconnaissance aircraft, in which role it remained until the summer of 1961.*

Below. *The Lockheed Hercules medium transport is widely used by the RAF today in a tactical role.*

efficient, maintaining a high state of readiness. The American intermediate range ballistic missile, Thor, was deployed in Bomber Command from 1958 to 1963, also as part of the overall deterrent. In 1960 the new Ballistic Missile Early Warning Station at Fylingdales Moor, Yorkshire, was announced, to become operational in 1963, to provide at least four minutes warning of a ballistic missile attack on the UK by the Soviet Union. Techniques were developed in Bomber Command for 'scrambling' dispersed detachments of the V-force swiftly enough – in less than four minutes – to ensure that massive retaliation for any nuclear attack could take place, thus ensuring that the 'deterrent' really deterred. At the Farnborough Air Show in September 1960, the RAF demonstrated scrambles by four of each of the three V-bombers (Valiants, Vulcans and Victors), with an average scramble time of 1 minute 47 seconds.

It was planned to prolong the effective line of the V-force by the acquisition of the American-developed Skybolt air-launched ballistic missile, to succeed the British Blue Steel stand-off nuclear weapon. But the US Government itself decided to cancel development of Skybolt for the US Air Force in December 1962,

The Avro Vulcan four-engined heavy bomber was the first large bomber in the world to use the 'Delta' wing plan-form. The prototype first flew on 30 August 1952, and the first production aircraft flew on 4 February 1955. Entering service with the Bomber Command Operational Conversion Unit on 22 February 1957, at Waddington, the Vulcan became fully operational with No. 83 Squadron in July of that year. As one of the famous 'triad' of V-bombers, the Vulcan carried the British strategic nuclear deterrent for many years, but eventually, on the advent of the Polaris nuclear missile carrying submarines, the aircraft assumed a tactical strike role, and is still in service today.

Above. *The last of the 'triad' of V-bombers to enter service, the Handley Page Victor long range aircraft B-1, joined the RAF in late 1957. When the later B-2 version was introduced, the B-1s were converted to the aerial tanker refuelling role. The B/SR-2 version was the RAF's standard strategic reconnaissance aircraft, which could map with radar an area of 750,000 square miles in six hours. Today, all the Victors in RAF service are converted for use as airborne tankers.*

Right. *The de Havilland Vampire was one of the earliest jet fighters to be developed.*

thereby also depriving the RAF of this weapon. Instead, under the Anglo-American Nassau agreement, it was decided that the eventual replacement of the air-launched nuclear deterrent would be a force of four British-built nuclear-powered missile-carrying submarines, using US-designed Polaris missiles. These would take several years to build, however, so that the deterrent role rested with the RAF through to 1969, when the Polaris force became operational. At that date, the UK-based V-bombers were transferred to the tactical role, although remaining assigned to NATO.

During much of the first 25 years of the post-war period, the RAF also maintained a substantial presence throughout the world: in the Mediterranean, in Malta and Cyprus; in the Middle East the RAF was stationed at Aden; in the Far East in Hong Kong, and in South-East Asia in Singapore, with other units in such places as Gan in the Maldive Islands in the Indian Ocean and on Masirah, south of the Gulf. Progressively, however, these overseas stations and garrisons were to be reduced as successive governments decided to withdraw for both political and economic reasons, and as more and more former British territories became

Perhaps the most famous of all post-war jet fighters in the RAF, the Hawker Hunter has been in continuous service in a number of roles from 1954 until the present day. Over 1,000 of these single-engined transonic fighters were built for export to overseas air forces. Although phased out of Fighter Command with the advent of the Lightning and the Canberra in 1962, the Hunter has remained in service in limited numbers in a tactical weapons training role.

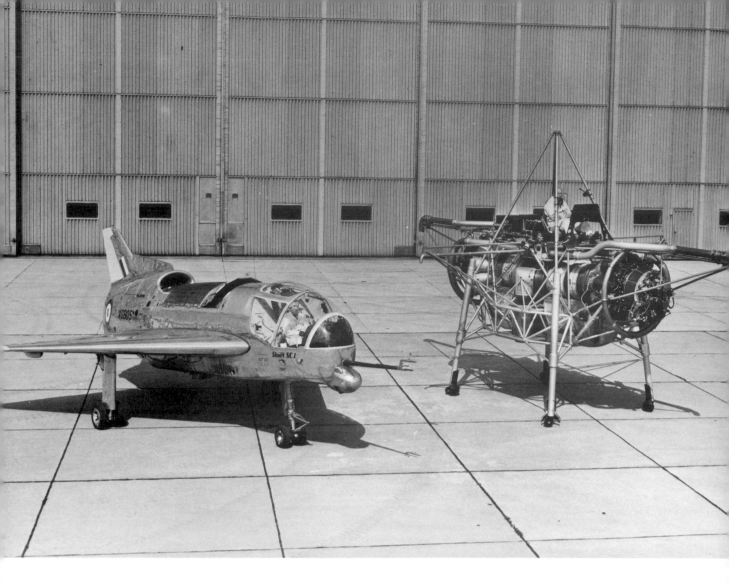

SC1 VTOL and Flying Bedstead. A new dimension, vertical take-off and landing, was added to aviation by the Rolls-Royce Flying Bedstead (right) which proved the feasibility of jet born vertical lift and control in 1953. The powered Bedstead is seen with the Short SC1 which employed four RB108 engines for lift, and one for propulsion.

independent and responsible for their own security.

During the 1950s and 1960s, the RAF was involved in a number of major operations overseas. These included actions against the terrorists in Malaya from 1948 to 1960; support in the Korean War in the early 1950s; against the Mau Mau in Kenya in 1954; in Cyprus against Eoka (the movement for union with Greece); in Aden and in the confrontation with Indonesia. The RAF also played a role in support of United Nations' operations in the Congo. One further important operation was at Suez, in 1956, when British and French forces invaded Egypt following the take-over by Colonel Nasser of the Suez Canal. In that operation, although politically abortive, the RAF played a major role in neutralising the Egyptian air force.

As part of the overall support operation for these substantial overseas activities, the RAF was equipped progressively with a major force of transport aircraft, initially through Transport Command, (subsequently to become Air Support Command and eventually to be absorbed into Strike Command). In June 1956,

the world's first all-jet transport aircraft squadron was formed with the introduction of Comet airliners to No. 216 Squadron at Lyneham, Wiltshire. The Britannia turbo-prop airliner entered service with No. 99 Squadron at Lyneham in June 1959. Later, the force was supplemented by the Argosy transport in 1961, the Belfast strategic long-range heavy fighter and the VC-10 long-range jet transport, both in 1966, and by the Hercules transport in 1967.

It was in this period also, due to the need to maintain a constant flow of aircraft between the UK and the widely-spread bases and activities overseas, that the RAF developed the technique of in-flight refuelling, first with Valiant tankers and then with Victors. This has also subsequently proved of immense value in enabling the UK Air Defence fighters to patrol for long periods over the North Atlantic to intercept Soviet intruders into UK and NATO airspace.

By 1952, the RAF was flying its post-war peak total of some 6,338 aircraft, and a year later it was at a personnel strength of 277,125 men and women, its highest in the post-war period.

P-1127 Kestrel – the early version of the Harrier undergoing tethered tests.

14 The Passing of The World Role
1957–1970

WHILE BOMBER COMMAND was carrying the responsibility of the nuclear deterrent, and other parts of the service were undertaking extensive operations in many parts of the world, the political pattern of the world itself was changing. This was to lead to a steady withdrawal by the British back to western Europe, with consequent effects upon the size and role of the RAF, and on the equipment it used.

The problems of re-equipment emerged quickly after the end of the War. In a decision that seems utterly astonishing today, the Government of the day decided soon after the end of the War not to embark upon the development of supersonic military aircraft, on the grounds not only that such aircraft would be too expensive, but also that they were likely to be unnecessary. This decision, much criticised at that time, undoubtedly caused the UK to fall behind in the development of single-seat supersonic fighters, and the lead so painstakingly built up by people like Whittle and his team was sacrificed to the USA.

It was not until it became apparent that the Soviet Union, as well as the USA, were pressing ahead rapidly with such aircraft, that the UK Government's decision was reversed, and work was begun on two types of high-speed fighter, the Hunter and the Swift. The Hunter proved the better of the two, being supersonic at sea level, and it became the RAF's standard single seat fighter, with over 1,000 being supplied to the service in several variants from July 1954 onwards, only being superseded by the English Electric Lightning in 1960 (the RAF's first truly supersonic jet fighter). Many Hunters remained in service and some are still used by the RAF for training purposes today. The Swift was less successful, and only went into service in small numbers in early 1954, being withdrawn from Fighter Command in 1955. The Gloster Javelin entered service in February 1956.

The difficulties began to emerge in the late 1950s. Efforts by

The Avro Vulcan B1 bomber, equipped with the Blue Steel stand-off bomb.

the Government in the Defence White Paper of 1957 to downgrade the development and use of manned military aircraft especially in Fighter Command, in favour of much greater use of guided missiles, found no support with the RAF. A sustained campaign by the Air Staff, however, effectively ensured that this policy was modified, in favour of the continued development of new military aircraft types.

Some severe shocks still lay ahead, however. One of the new types of aircraft which the Air Staff had initially been able to retain in development against pressures for cancellation was the TSR-2 tactical-strike-reconnaissance aircraft, which the RAF regarded at that time as the lynch-pin for its future operational activities. Although the aircraft first flew in September 1964, however, it was destined never to enter service. Because of the call for further massive reductions in defence spending by the new Labour Government in late 1964 and early 1965, and the decision to expedite the withdrawal from many of Britain's overseas possessions and to concentrate her forces upon NATO and Western Europe, the TSR-2 was cancelled in the Budget speech in the spring of 1965. Earlier in that year, the Government had also cancelled both the P-1154 vertical take-off supersonic interceptor

Above. *A Victor scramble at RAF Cottesmore in 1969. The Air Electronics Officer leads, he has switches to throw before the Captain can start the engines. Last is the Navigator who shuts the door.*

Right. *A Vulcan aircraft of No. 83 Squadron being serviced.*

and ground attack aircraft (in favour of buying a number of Phantom jet fighters from the USA). The Hawker Siddeley HS-681 short-take-off and landing transport aircraft was also cancelled and Britain purchased Hercules freighters, also from the USA.

These decisions not only hit the RAF hard, but also caused considerable dismay in the aerospace manufacturing industry. In 1966, it was decided to buy up to 50 General Dynamics F-111 swing-wing fighter-bombers from the US, as Canberra replacements. This decision was also subsequently cancelled, early in 1968, when the Defence White Paper in the early spring of that year announced further sweeping defence cuts, including the withdrawal from the Persian Gulf and the Far East by December 1971.

Due to the progressive withdrawal from long-established territories and bases overseas, the RAF itself was shrinking. One result of this was that in the Defence White Paper of 1967, it was announced that Bomber and Fighter Commands would merge in April 1968, to form a new Command, later named Strike Command. Eventually, 'Strike', as it came to be called, would also take over Coastal Command, Signals Command and Air Support (formerly Transport) Command.

The catalogue of cuts and shrinkage continued through the 1960s. In the 1968 Defence White Paper, it was announced that large aircraft carriers were to be phased out, and certain Naval aircraft, such as the Buccaneers, were to be transferred to the RAF, while at the same time, the number of active personnel in the Service was to be run down at a faster rate over the ensuing five years.

There were some consolations, however, in what was a most unhappy period for the RAF. One aircraft type, later to perform valuable service, which survived despite the spate of cuts, was the Hawker P-1127 Kestrel (later named the Harrier) vertical take-off fighter, the first of its kind in the world. The Harrier entered service with No. 1 Squadron at Wittering in October 1969, at the same time as the Buccaneer strike aircraft joined the RAF, with

At the RAF Technical College, Henlow, cadets learn principles of flight systems and auto pilots using a 3-dimensional mock up which permits movement on 3 axes.

A Valiant refuelling a Vulcan.

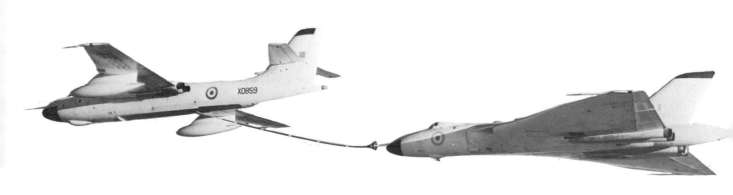

Overalled technicians perform static tests and fuelling on a Blue Steel stand-off bomb.

No. 12 Squadron at Honington. Although originally developed for the Royal Navy, the Buccaneer was transferred to the RAF when it was decided in the late 1960s to phase out big aircraft carriers.

The year 1969, by comparison with what had gone before, was almost a vintage year for the RAF in the number of new types of aircraft entering the squadrons. In addition to the Harrier and the Buccaneer, the American-built McDonnell Douglas Phantom fighter, one of the greatest jet fighters the world has seen, became operational with the RAF. Nimrod maritime reconnaissance aircraft, developed from the Comet jet airliner, entered service late in 1969 to replace the Shackletons in the maritime reconnaissance (anti-submarine warfare) role. The latter was becoming a major aspect of the RAF's work, on behalf of NATO, as awareness grew of the rapid build-up of the Soviet Union's submarine-construction programme.

Despite all the cuts and rundowns of the 1950s and 1960s, however, the RAF strove to remain a pioneering force, determined to continue the conquest of the skies begun so many years earlier. Not long after V-E day, on 26 May 1945, a Lancaster named

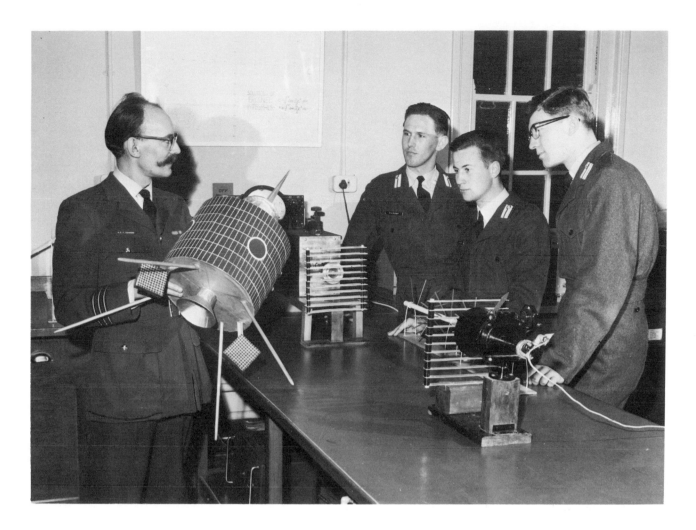

Cadets being taught polarization phenomena of satellite aerials.

Aries, from the Empire Air Navigation School, made the first British flight over the North Pole and North Magnetic Pole, with a stop at Whitehorse, Yukon, completing an eventual journey of 17,720 miles (28,517 km).

In 1951, the Canberra, a twin-jet bomber, entered service with No. 101 Squadron at Binbrook, and quickly established itself, like the Valiant, as one of the RAF's most versatile aircraft, setting many records and filling many roles. In October 1953 a Canberra flown by Flight Lieutenants R. L. E. Burton and D. H. Gannon won the Speed Section of the London–New Zealand air race, flying 12,220 miles (19,666 km) in 23 hours 50 minutes 42 seconds, establishing also many intermediate point-to-point records. This was the first of many long distance air records set by the RAF in the post-war era. They included the first direct trans-Atlantic flight by a Valiant V-bomber in September 1956, followed by an England–Melbourne flight by a Vulcan, covering 11,475 miles (18,467 km) in an elapsed time of 47 hours 26 minutes. With the aid of aerial refuelling, a Valiant of No. 214 Squadron, captained by Wing Commander M. J. Beetham, flew non-stop from the UK to Cape

Town in July 1959, a distance of 6,060 miles (9,753 km) in 11 hours 28 minutes. Also using aerial refuelling, in March 1960 a Valiant made the longest ever flight non-stop by an RAF aircraft, 8,500 miles (13,679 km) around the UK, in 18 hours 5 minutes.

The RAF was also pre-eminent in high-speed flight. On 7 November 1945, Group Captain H. J. 'Willie' Wilson, of the re-formed High Speed Flight, in a Meteor F. Mark III specially brought up to Mark IV standards, set a new World Absolute Air Speed Record of 606.26 mph (975.68 km/h), at Herne Bay, Kent. This was the first officially confirmed record established by a jet aircraft. On 7 September 1946, Group Captain E. M. 'Teddy' Donaldson, flying a Meteor F. Mark IV, put the record up again to 615.78 mph (991 km/h).

On 1 April 1968, the RAF celebrated the 50th anniversary of its foundation, but behind the ceremonial flag-waving and the bands playing, there were many in the service who wondered what the 1970s were to bring. The 1960s had been a time of severe trial for the RAF. It had seen its forces whittled down, some of its cherished aircraft programmes abandoned, and many of its traditional roles shorn away, as many of the stations and garrisons overseas closed down in the wake of the great British political withdrawal back to Europe.

At the same time, the technology of warfare itself had been changing rapidly, creating demands for new types of weapons, in terms of both aircraft and guided weapons, of increasing complexity and capability. New tactical and strategic concepts had to be evolved to meet all these changes, and the RAF was obliged to learn, as were other branches of the armed forces, that new political considerations prevailed in the world, requiring swift adaptation if the service was to survive.

The RAF had been created and nurtured against the background of an Imperial tradition, with the task of policing and preserving a Commonwealth and Empire. After the brief rearmament of the early 1950s, it had been obliged, throughout the 1960s, to stand by and watch a major run-down take place under the twin influences of economic stringency and political policies with which many in the country, as well as in the armed forces, disagreed. On the threshold of the 1970s, who could tell what lay ahead?

The Handley Page Victor was one of the RAF's famous 'triad' of V-bombers which included the Vickers Valiant and the Avro Vulcan.

The Era of Renewed Optimism

1970–1982 15

THE RAF HAS always been an adaptable and resilient service. It has had to be, under the influence of changing political requirements. At no time in its history was this shown to better advantage than during the 1970s. Many had feared at the end of the 1960s, with the transfer of the nuclear deterrent to the Royal Navy, the loss of many overseas bases and the loss of many cherished new aircraft programmes, that the RAF was likely to be downgraded into a third-rate service, of little real value to the nation.

In the event, the reverse was the case, for a number of reasons. The main effort was now concentrated on NATO. Although still required to operate under conditions of considerable financial stringency, with never enough aircraft to fulfill all its tasks in the way its commanders would have liked, the RAF nevertheless achieved a great deal during the 1970s. One of the principal factors behind its survival was the slow realisation, on the part of governments, after more than 25 years of peace in Europe, that the next war, if ever it came, would be fought more in terms of conventional weapons than of nuclear ones. While this did not obviate the need for a nuclear deterrent on the part of the Allies, including a continued UK contribution, it did mean that the massive cutbacks in conventional weapons that had disfigured the 1960s, had to be reversed. At the same time, it became clear that new concepts of organisation would be needed to meet changing circumstances, and that any new aircraft would have to combine many roles in order to be cost-effective in an era of soaring costs and continued budgetary stringency.

The result was, first, a reorganisation of the RAF itself, and, secondly, the development of new aircraft types capable of undertaking 'multi-roles' and even new tasks. In April 1968, Bomber and Fighter Commands had been merged to form a new Strike Command, taking in also Signals and Coastal Commands. Eventually Air Support Command which had been formed from

Air Chief Marshal Sir Andrew Humphrey, first Commander in Chief of Strike Command.

Opposite. The Anglo-West German-Italian Panavia Tornado swing-wing multi-role combat aircraft will be the mainstay of the RAF through the rest of the 1980s and beyond.

Transport Command was also engulfed, to provide transport and other support operations for the RAF in the field.

Strike Command was the spearhead of the RAF through the 1970s, operating and controlling the nuclear strike, conventional attack, strategic reconnaissance, air defence, long-range maritime reconnaissance and air-to-air refuelling forces, as well as all the elements of air power required for the immediate support of a force in the field. The new Command controlled a total of some 50,000 personnel and over 800 aircraft, which were assigned to either NATO's Supreme Allied Commander in Europe (SACEUR) or the Supreme Allied Commander Atlantic (SACLANT). The objective of creating the new Command was to ensure the most effective and economical use of the RAF's multi-role front-line force. The Command extended over the whole of the UK, from Saxa Vord in the Shetlands to St. Mawgan in Cornwall, as well as overseas. Its aircraft included the supersonic air defence Lightning fighters; the ground-attack and air defence Phantoms (which although bought from the US were equipped with Rolls-Royce Spey engines and much British equipment); the Buccaneer strike aircraft; the Jaguar tactical aircraft and the Harrier vertical take-off aircraft.

Opposite. *Now on order for the RAF is the Advanced Version of the Harrier vertical take-off fighter, the AV-8B, being developed jointly by British Aerospace and McDonnell Douglas of the USA. Shown here is the prototype AV-8B in the colours of the US Marine Corps, who will also use the aircraft.*

Above. *The multi-role Tornado aircraft will also be used by the RAF in its basic or 'Interdictor Strike' version (IDS), capable of a wide range of tasks.*

Page 156 top. *The British Aerospace (originally Hawker Siddeley) Andover twin-engined tactical transport aircraft is one of the 'workhorses' of the RAF.*

Page 156 bottom. *A Rolls-Royce Spey-powered Phantom fighter was used to commemorate the 60th anniversary in 1979 of the 1919 transatlantic non-stop flight by Alcock and Brown in a Rolls-Royce Eagle-powered Vickers Vimy bomber.*

Page 157. *A Sea King of the RAF Search and Rescue Services.*

Strike Command also had Shackleton Airborne Early Warning (AEW) aircraft; the Vulcan bombers in a long-range tactical strike role; the giant VC-10 jet transports; the Belfast wide-bodied turbo-prop freighter; the Nimrod maritime reconnaissance jet; the Victor bombers converted to a tanker role; the smaller but ubiquitous Hercules transport, and various helicopters, such as the Puma tactical support aircraft.

Strike Command, with its headquarters at High Wycombe, consisted of five operational groups in the early 1970s (although in November 1975, this was reduced to four, with the amalgamation of Nos. 38 and 46 groups to become No. 38 Group).

No. 1 Group was responsible for the day-to-day operational control and training of the strike/attack, air-to-air refuelling and reconnaissance forces. No. 11 Group similarly controlled the air defence squadrons of Lightnings and Phantoms with their associated communications and ground environment radars, including the Ballistic Missile Early Warning Station at Fylingdales. No. 18 Group was responsible for long-range maritime reconnaissance, anti-submarine warfare, and for Search and Rescue. No. 38 Group was responsible for UK ground attack, helicopters and RAF Regiment squadrons and the tactical communications wing. Through No. 46 Group, with its strategic transport aircraft, Strike Command was also responsible for the support and protection of the few remaining British territories and the Allies' friends outside

An RAF Buccaneer low level bomber.

Europe. This called for the ability to deploy and support both ground and air forces in various parts of the world at short notice. This was achieved using VC-10s for long-range transport, the Belfast freighters for a wide range of bulky loads, the 'work-horse' and very versatile Hercules, and short-range transports such as Andovers, while the older Britannia turbo-prop and Comet jet airliners were used for long-range scheduled service operations. No. 46 Group also operated the Queen's Flight, based at RAF Benson.

During the early 1970s especially, the UK still maintained some overseas defence installations – in Hong Kong, Singapore, and Cyprus, with staging posts at Gan in the Maldives in the Indian Ocean and at Masirah, at the foot of the Gulf in the Arabian Sea. In Oman, the RAF kept a detachment at Salalah airfield, the base of the Sultan of Oman's Air Force, which included some RAF personnel on loan.

Thus, through the 1970s, the RAF was remoulded, until it became substantially – though not entirely – what it is today. The aircraft in service through the 1970s are substantially the same as those today – the Lightnings and Phantoms, Buccaneers, Jaguars,

Harrier VTOL aircraft, Victors in the tanker role, and Vulcans in the tactical long-range strike role, along with VC-10s and Hercules transports, Nimrods for maritime reconnaissance and Airborne Early Warning duties, and various helicopters.

There was one major difference, however, between the RAF of the 1970s and what had gone before. The service had undergone what was called a 'hardware revolution', in which one single aircraft had become capable of depositing on an enemy an immensely greater payload of weapons, even nuclear weapons if necessary. At the outbreak of the 1914–1918 war, the flimsy military aeroplanes of the Royal Flying Corps and the Royal Naval Air Service were experimenting with new aerial mines and grenades to use against enemy airships and ground forces. It was thought then that up to 40 lbs. (18.14 kg) of explosives could be dropped from a height of 350 feet (107 m), without damage to the aircraft. To launch smaller weapons the pilot or observer leaned over the side of the cockpit, and literally dropped the lethal devices from his grasp.

During the Second World War, the size of bombs increased, until by the end of the war, the 'Grand Slam' of 22,000 lbs. (9,979 kg) was a regular load for the heavy Lancaster bombers.

Westland/Aerospatiale SA 330 – Puma. An Odiham-based Puma helicopter flies low over the countryside near its home base. Note the de-icing air intakes for all-weather operation.

By the 1970s, however, one RAF strike fighter alone could deliver a bomb load of 16,000 lbs. (7,257 kg) on to a moving target with pin-point accuracy. With the development of new techniques of target acquisition and identification, such as laser range-finders, together with improved navigational equipment such as the Inertial Navigation System, the ability of modern fighter and bomber aircraft to find and destroy their targets was immensely improved beyond anything that could have been imagined even during the Second World War.

The extraordinary progress also made in the development of nuclear weapons, moreover, made it possible for even a fighter aircraft to carry such weapons if necessary, so that although the modern Royal Air Force is substantially smaller in numbers of aircraft than at any time since the end of the Second World War, its destructive capability has been multiplied many scores of times, and will be multiplied even further in the years ahead.

One major development initiated in the 1970s, only now

Above. *An RAF Hercules C Mk I from RAF Lyneham is seen on the apron at Barbados airport after unloading supplies for the Dominican disaster relief.*

Opposite. *A Nimrod MR Mk 2 of No. 206 Squadron RAF Kinloss, seen in the new 'Hemp' camouflage, flying over an oil rig in the Moray Firth.*

The Jetstream is a twin engined pilot-trainer used by the RAF and the Navy for communications purposes.

coming to fruition, was the three-nation (British, West German and Italian) multi-role combat aircraft, the Tornado. This formidable aircraft is intended to take over many of the roles performed by existing ageing aircraft – in counter-air and interdiction operations (penetrating behind enemy lines using conventional weapons to destroy airfields, lines of communications and other installations), nuclear strike, reconnaissance and air defence. The RAF is buying 385 of these aircraft, out of the total of 809 on order (including 100 for Italy and 324 for West Germany), of which 165 will be of the specialist 'Air Defence Variant' or ADV, for the Air Defence of the UK, while the other 220 will be the IDS (Interdictor Strike) version for the wide range of other roles mentioned. The Tornado is one of the best things that has happened to the RAF during the 1970s, and will comprise the backbone of the force through the 1980s and beyond.

The RAF Today and Into The Future 16

DESPITE SUCCESSIVE CUTS in defence spending and the closure of many overseas bases, the RAF remains a substantial force, and it has retained all of its traditional air power roles. It is still a very crucial element in the UK's overall defence posture, and is likely to remain so certainly through to the end of this century and into the next.

With a front-line force of 52 aircraft squadrons and eight missile squadrons, involving 93,500 personnel, the RAF today has a number of major tasks. Primarily, it is required to contribute tactical strike forces in support of the nuclear deterrent (which is currently in the hands of the Navy's Polaris missile-carrying submarines and is ultimately to be replaced by the Trident system). At the same time, it must provide an offensive air capability; battlefield support in Central Europe; provide for the air defence of the UK itself and provide land-based maritime support for operations in the Eastern Atlantic. To achieve these tasks the majority of the front line aircraft are either directly assigned to NATO's Supreme Allied Commander Europe (SACEUR) or Supreme Allied Commander Atlantic (SACLANT), or are earmarked to them in time of need. Some of the RAF's training aircraft, such as Hawks, which are being equipped with Sidewinder air-to-air missiles to give them a combat role for local air defence, will also form part of the UK air defence forces.

In effect, this means that some of the front-line squadrons, notably many of the air defence fighter aircraft, missiles and radars are assigned to SACEUR all the time. UK air defence aircraft, for example, are under the Commander-in-Chief, Strike Command, in his NATO appointment of Commander-in-Chief United Kingdom Air Forces (CINCUKAIR). The majority of other units not assigned in this way remain under national control in peacetime, only coming under SACEUR or SACLANT in time of tension or war.

The RAF's tasks today can be conveniently listed under several headings: Nuclear Strike and Conventional Attack; Offensive Support in Europe; Air Defence of the UK; Maritime Support; and Other Roles (such as transport, support of British forces based overseas, training, search and rescue and ground defence).

For Strike and Attack, the RAF has six squadrons of long-range tactical Vulcan bombers, that were originally built for the strategic role when the RAF was responsible for the nuclear deterrent before that was passed to the Royal Navy. Amounting to about 50 aircraft, the Vulcan force can carry free-fall nuclear bombs, and in this role can penetrate well behind the battlefield against the deeper targets beyond the range of the majority of tactical aircraft available to NATO. But because the Vulcans are now ageing, it is intended that they will be replaced by the Tornado multi-role combat aircraft in its Interdictor Strike (IDS) version.

Above. *The latest RAF Helicopter – the Boeing Vertol Chinook medium support helicopter, capable of lifting 10 tons of equipment or 43 troops.*

Opposite. *The Royal Air Force Search and Rescue Service. A Wessex helicopter is working in conjunction with Her Majesty's Air Force Vessel* Seal, *a long range recovery and support craft based at Alness, Scotland.*

A GR1 Jaguar carrying two 1,200 litre fuel tanks and four 1,000 lb bombs.

This re-equipment has already started and the total of 220 Tornado GR-1s to be bought will ultimately replace not only the Vulcan but also the Canberra and the Buccaneer. In addition to the nuclear strike role, the Tornado GR-1 will be required to penetrate behind the enemy's lines to attack airfields, using the JP-233 airfield denial weapon, as well as bridges, supply depots, troop concentrations and other tactically important targets. To meet these tasks the Tornado GR-1 is fitted with an advanced terrain-following system to enable it to fly supersonically over even the roughest country under the enemy's radar cover by day or night, and in all weather conditions.

For strike/attack, offensive support and reconnaissance in Europe, RAF Germany contributes nine fast jet squadrons to NATO's Second Tactical Air Force, together with one Puma (changing to Chinook) helicopter squadron for logistic support. This total force is made up of two Buccaneer, four Jaguar and two

Harrier vertical/short take-off squadrons together with a single Jaguar reconnaissance squadron. The whole force is complemented by a further two squadrons of Phantoms for air defence over Northern Germany. In addition to the German-based squadrons, Jaguars, Harriers, Wessex and Pumas drawn from 38 Group's units in the United Kingdom contribute to NATO's Ace Mobile Force and other 'contingency' plans within the European theatre. The Buccaneers and Jaguars, although they can be given tasks of selective air attack in the strike role with nuclear weapons, are primarily designed to disrupt the movement of enemy forces behind the battlefield. Harriers are primarily intended for close battlefield support, giving the field commanders heavy fire power against tanks and armoured vehicles.

The RAF's forces in the Central Region of NATO also include one squadron of Bloodhound and four squadrons of Rapier ground-to-air missiles for anti-aircraft defence, and one squadron

The Hercules C Mk 3 was the first 'stretched' Hercules delivered to the Royal Air Force. The aircraft has been stretched by 15 feet. This photograph shows the first stage in the dropping of a 7 ton load attached to a cluster of 3 parachutes.

of the RAF Regiment for the ground-defence of airfields and other installations. In all, the RAF has some 150 Jaguars, over 100 Harriers and about 60 Buccaneers.

The third major task for the RAF is the Air Defence of the UK. The Soviet Union has over 500 medium/heavy bombers available for attack on the UK, and is adding to this total every year. Some of them, such as the supersonic Backfire bomber, have sufficient range to be able to fly down through the Greenland–Iceland Gap into the North Atlantic, to attack the UK and Western Europe from the 'back door'. Thus, the first objective of the RAF is to detect such infiltration, which it does with one squadron of Shackleton Airborne Early Warning (AEW) aircraft. These patrol far out into the North Atlantic for many hours at a time, supported by high-powered ground-based radars around the coasts.

Once detected and identified, there are five squadrons of Phantoms and two of Lightnings kept at a high stage of readiness in the UK to intercept the intruders. Hardly a day goes by without some of these jets being 'scrambled' to make interceptions far out over the Atlantic. These interceptions average about five every week, and on most occasions the fighters are supported by Victor air-to-air refuelling tankers. Although the end-result of an interception is normally 'shadowing', as the aircraft proceeds along its route, the Phantoms and Lightnings are armed for hostilities if necessary.

The AEW Shackletons are soon to be replaced by the new AEW version of the Nimrod, which although developed from the maritime reconnaissance Nimrod, contains totally new detection equipment for its air defence role. Eleven AEW Nimrods are planned.

The AEW Nimrods will form part of the new sophisticated system known as the UK Air Defence Ground Environment (UKADGE) which is now under development and will include new and more sophisticated radars and communication systems to improve the detection capability against these Soviet movements. Further improvements will shortly also include an additional VC-10 tanker squadron to supplement the existing two squadrons of Victors, and eventually, the air defence Phantoms and Lightnings will be replaced by the Air Defence Variant of Tornado. Of these, 165 aircraft are being bought, and to strengthen the total force they will be supplemented by the retention in service of two squadrons of Phantoms.

Behind the fighter screen, Bloodhound and Rapier surface-to-air missiles provide a further line of defence. Rapier gives cover at short-range against low-level air attack, while the Bloodhound gives medium-range area protection. But a new medium range missile for ground-to-air defence is needed for the future, and it is

hoped that this can be developed in the 1980s in conjunction with our Allies.

The RAF is also responsible for contributing to the maritime defence of the Western Sea approaches to NATO, which includes the sea lanes leading to United Kingdom ports. For this purpose, four squadrons of Nimrod long-range maritime patrol aircraft are available for the detection and destruction of enemy submarines and surface ships. These aircraft can range far out into the North Atlantic, to detect enemy submarines.

Shore-based air defence cover for the Royal Navy is provided by two squadrons of RAF Phantoms while two squadrons of Buccaneers, armed with Martel anti-radar and TV guided missiles as well as laser-guided bombs, provide the anti-shipping capability.

The range and endurance of aircraft operating in both the air defence and anti-shipping roles can be greatly extended by the use of RAF air-to-air tankers. Although both the Buccaneers and Phantoms will ultimately be replaced in these roles by both variants of Tornado, two Buccaneer squadrons will continue in the anti-shipping role into the 1990s.

Of the many other roles, air transport provides the flexibility and rapid deployment so necessary for modern fighting forces. The RAF is equipped in all with one squadron of VC-10 long-range transports, and four squadrons of Hercules medium-range transports, together with Wessex and Puma helicopter squadrons in the UK and a Chinook medium lift squadron in Germany.

The RAF also provides support for UK forces outside NATO with one Whirlwind/Wessex helicopter squadron and one squadron of the RAF Regiment in Cyprus, one squadron of Wessex

Above. An artist's impression of a VC-10 Tanker in-flight refuelling two Tornados.

Page 172. An RAF aerial rigger at work. Before acceptance trainee riggers must climb a 300 foot radio mast to prove they have no fear of heights.

Page 173. The Royal Air Force Regiment undertakes its share of ceremonial duties. Here the Regiment is seen on Royal Guard duties at Buckingham Palace.

British Aerospace Hawk trainers from RAF Station Chivenor. The RAF has 176 Hawks in service, in a variety of roles ranging from training and light combat to service with the famous Red Arrows aerobatic team.

Opposite above. *The jet-powered British Aerospace Nimrod long-range maritime reconnaissance aircraft was developed from the original Comet jet airliner.*

Above. *Members of the RAF Regiment learning unarmed combat.*

Opposite below. *The Nimrod has subsequently also been developed into a more specialised Airborne Early Warning aircraft.*

Air Training Corps Cadets fixing the launching winch to a glider.

helicopters in Hong Kong (where they help the Hong Kong Government in controlling the illegal immigrant problem), and a detachment of Harrier jump-jets and Puma helicopters in Belize, together with a Rapier missile air defence unit.

With the complexity and high cost of modern aircraft, training of both aircrew and ground-crew is vitally important to the RAF. For the advanced stage of pilot training, the RAF has a force of 176 British Aerospace Hawk trainers in service. Some of these are also capable of using Sidewinder air-to-air missiles to allow for their use in a local air defence role.

The RAF's Search and Rescue duties round Britain's coasts have become famous, and the daring exploits of the helicopter crews in atrocious weather are part of the S & R units' daily lives. Two squadrons, made up of Sea Kings, Wessex and Whirlwind helicopters, in 1980 rescued 834 people in 1,173 missions, many of them under conditions in which surface ships could not have done the job.

Finally, there is the ground defence of the RAF's airfields and other installations within NATO, which is entrusted to four

Above. *Advanced Training of pilots with a tactical Hawk. Trainee pilots graduate from Bulldog to Jet Provost and thence to fly Hawks. At the end of this Hawk training they get their wings. Fast jet pilots then go on to learn tactical weapons firing from this kind of Hawk.*

Left. *Airmen clothed in protective NBC (nuclear, biological and chemical) clothing servicing a Harrier aircraft in the field.*

Above. *WRAF Fighter Controllers watching radar screens at RAF West Drayton.*

Right. *WRAF safety equipment workers loading parachutes.*

Above. *Operations room briefing for aircrew.*

Left. *Airmen guarding a Harrier landing strip.*

squadrons of the RAF Regiment in the UK and one in Germany, together with three squadrons of the Royal Auxiliary Air Force.

All of these roles may not remain the same indefinitely, for the RAF, like the Navy and the Army, is required to be adaptable in the light of ever-changing political, economic, military and other circumstances. As we have seen throughout this survey of the first seventy years of military flying in Britain, changes in the circumstances of the RAF and its predecessors, the RFC and RNAS, as indeed even with the original Balloon Companies and Balloon School of the Royal Engineers before and after the turn of the

Above. *Wessex helicopters exercising in Norway, part of the annual NATO manoeuvres.*

Opposite. *RAF Regiment gunners training with the Tiger Cat Missile.*

Above. *Training for another part of the RAF Rescue Services – Mountain Rescue.*

Right. *RAF Firemen are ready to cope with any emergency after training of this kind, another duty of the RAF Regiment.*

RAF Central Band playing for a display by the Queen's Colour Squadron.

century, were almost a *sine qua non* of the service. As a result, it has built up an expectation of and readiness to change, and an ability to achieve miracles often in the face of almost insuperable odds, often with the minimum of equipment. The RAF, in this respect, reflects the innate character of the British people.

It is already clear that there will be further changes in the future. New aircraft will be required – for example, replacements for the Jaguar jet strike-trainer aircraft, and for the Harrier vertical take-off fighter – and new concepts of warfare are also likely to emerge.

It is now widely recognised, not only by the West, but also by the Warsaw Pact forces, that air power is paramount – a lesson that has been reinforced time and again in the past few years (for example, in the Arab–Israeli wars), and which became apparent during the Second World War in many different theatres. Command of the air is essential to the command of the battle, and thus of the war. Lose control of the air, and the battle – and the war – are lost. The RAF has an essential role to play in the overall UK

Opposite. An RAF police dog with his handler guarding a low level Air Defence Missile Site.

A Jaguar aircraft outside a hardened aircraft shelter in Germany.

defence posture. It is simply because of this fact that very large sums are being spent on re-equipping it. The decisions contained in the Defence Review of June 1981, implicitly recognised the need to strengthen the RAF and particularly the air defence of the UK.

Looking back over the past seventy years, at the progression from balloons, man-carrying kites and airships through to the Tornado multi-role combat aircraft of today, it is astonishing to recall all that has been achieved. No-one knows what the future holds. Although geared for war – and nuclear war at that – the RAF, like everyone else in these islands, hopes that it will never come, and that the deterrent strength of Britain, vested in its armed forces, does successfully deter the potential enemy from making any pre-emptive strike. But, should that day dawn, the RAF, as throughout the past seventy years, can be expected to give of its best in the defence of the United Kingdom.

Bibliography

The bibliography given below represents only a proportion of the many sources consulted – books, newspapers, magazines, historical documents, etc. The books included herein, however, constitute a reasonably comprehensive list of follow-up reading for those interested in the history of the RAF and the RFC, and in aeronautical history generally, over the past seventy years.

Banks, Air Commodore F. R., *I Kept No Diary*. Airlife Publications, Shrewsbury, 1978.

Barker, Ralph, *The Schneider Trophy Races*. Chatto & Windus, London, 1971.

Barnes, C. H., *Shorts Aircraft Since 1900*. Putnam, London, 1967.

Bowyer, Chaz, *Air War Over Europe. 1939–45*. William Kimber, London, 1981.

Bowyer, Chaz, *History of the RAF, 1912–1917*. Hamlyn, London, 1981.

Collier, Basil, *A History of Air Power*. Weidenfeld and Nicolson, London, 1974.

Dean, Sir Maurice, *The Royal Air Force in Two World Wars*. Cassell, London, 1979.

Gibbs-Smith, C. H., *The Aeroplane, An Historical Survey*. Science Museum (HMSO), London, 1960 (and revised and expanded edition, 1970).

Gibson, Wing Commander Guy, *Enemy Coast Ahead*. Michael Joseph, London, 1946.

Harker, R. W., *Rolls-Royce From The Wings, 1925–1971*. Oxford Illustrated Press, 1976.

Harris, Marshal of the RAF Sir Arthur, *Bomber Offensive*. Collins, London, 1947.

Jackson, A. J., *Blackburn Aircraft Since 1909*. Putnam, London, 1968.

James, Derek N., *Gloster Aircraft Since 1917*. Putnam, London, 1971.

Jane's All the World's Aircraft (annual editions), Macdonald & Co.

Jones, Neville, *The Origins of Strategic Bombing*. Wm. Kimber, London, 1973.

Joubert, Air Chief Marshal Sir Philip, *The Third Service*. Thames & Hudson, London, 1955.

Lewis, Peter, *The British Bomber Since 1914*. Putnam, London, 1967.

Penrose, Harald, *British Aviation, The Pioneer Years, 1903–1914*. Putnam, London, 1967.

Penrose, Harald, *British Aviation: The Great War and the Armistice, 1915–1919*. Putnam, London, 1969.

Penrose, Harald, *British Aviation, The Adventuring Years, 1920–1929*. Putnam, London, 1973.

Penrose, Harald, *British Aviation, Widening Horizons, 1930–1934*. Royal Air Force Museum (HMSO) London, 1979.

Reed, Arthur, and Turnill, Reginald, *Farnborough, The Story of the Royal Aircraft Establishment*. Robert Hale, London, 1980.

Richey, Paul, *Fighter Pilot*. Batsford, London, 1941.

Richards and Saunders, *The RAF, 1939–1945* (three volumes). HMSO, London, 1953–1954.

Robertson, Bruce, *Sopwith, The Man and His Aircraft*. Air Review, Letchworth, 1970.

Strong, Colin, and Hart-Davis, Duff, *Fighter Pilot*. Queen Anne Press and BBC, London, 1981.

Tapper, Oliver, *Roots In The Sky*. IPC Business Press, London, 1980.

Taylor, John W. R., and Munson, Kenneth (Eds.), *History of Aviation*. New English Libary, London, 1972.

Time-Life Books: *The Epic of Flight*. Time-Life International, London, 1981.

Thetford, Owen, *Aircraft of the Royal Air Force Since 1918*. Putnam, London, 1957.

Turner, Michael, *The RAF: Aircraft In Service Since 1918*. Hamlyn, London, 1981.

Walker, Percy B., *Early Aviation at Farnborough*. Macdonald & Co., London, 1971.

Webster & Frankland, *The Strategic Air Offensive Over Germany*. HMSO (four volumes), 1961.

Wood, Derek, *Project Cancelled*. Macdonald & Jane's, London, 1975.

Wood, Derek, and Dempster, Derek, *The Narrow Margin, The Battle of Britain and the Rise of Air Power*. Hutchinson, London, 1961.

Index

(figures in italics indicate reference to pictures)